Russell Potts, like many others, sailed model boats as a boy, but laid them aside at a relatively early age. He trained as a historian and spent his working life in and around the Ministry of Defence.

He returned to model yachting in the early 1970s and for several years was an active, if not very successful, competitor in radio controlled racing at national and international level. He served on the Council of the Model Yachting Association, eventually as General Secretary. He also played a major part in the organisation of World Championships held in Britain in 1986 and 1990.

Since retiring from competitive sailing, he has been studying the history of the sport. In 1987 he founded the Vintage Model Yacht Group, of which he is now Chairman. He is also a member of the British Society of Sports History and was the founding editor of its journal, *The Sports Historian*.

A comprehensive study of the history of model yachting is to be published at an uncertain future date.

Paul Croxson trained initially in the public library service, but then worked for many years as an international trader. Subsequently he joined Maggs Brothers, the antiquarian booksellers, where he is currently Company Secretary.

His interest in model boats came late in life and he has no history of competitive sailing. As he disdains the use of radio, his sailing is gradually becoming less active, and he devotes much effort to the restoration of his collection of boats. He hopes eventually to own a copy of every available book on the subject of model yachting. Collecting in so limited a field, this may not be a totally impossible ambition, though the discoveries that have been made in the course of compiling the present work have substantially increased the distance to the finishing line.

GW01057576

A
BIBLIOGRAPHY
OF
MODEL YACHTING

BY
RUSSELL POTTS
AND
PAUL CROXSON

ISBN : 1 873148 10 0

THE CURVED AIR PRESS
8 SHERARD ROAD
LONDON SE9 6EP

CONTENTS

INTRODUCTION

The aim of this book is to survey the printed materials from which the history of model yachting may be reconstructed. It is addressed to all those interested in the history of the sport and the models with which it has been pursued, and particularly the members of the Vintage Model Yacht Group and its American counterpart, the US Vintage Model Yacht Group. It has grown out of a checklist of older 'how to do it' titles prepared for members of the Vintage Group and has been expanded to cover all known titles that deal with model sailing boats.

There is also information which we believe will be of value to historians of sport and leisure, who have, so far, tended to ignore model sports and, since model yachting is essentially a technological sport, to historians of technology. Though it clearly contains much information that will be superfluous to their requirements, we hope it will also prove of value to booksellers and librarians.

That said, it has to be recognised that it is a deeply self-indulgent production, reflecting the obsessions of its authors, and delving deep into a literature that is in large part trivial, if entertaining.

It should also perhaps be explained that the bulk of the writing, both of the introduction and of the commentary, is by Russell Potts. Paul Croxson has made a smaller, but important contribution, as have the various collectors noted in the acknowledgements.

Scope

The primary focus is upon the organised sport of model yachting, conducted with practical sailing boats, what were once memorably described by a yachting journal, desperately seeking to avoid calling them 'toy boats', as 'unmanned wind powered vehicles'.[1]

While there is a relatively small number of titles that deal authoritatively with model yachting as a serious, organised sport for adults, there are many more that deal more generally with sailing models of various types and a further large fringe of short treatments contained in books covering general modelling topics or in compendia on hobbies and amusements. A very wide range of periodicals has from time to time given coverage to the sport. Some of these have been ephemeral, others extremely long lived. In

---

1 The antique trade, which remains invincibly ignorant of what model yachts are for, other than interior decoration, characterises them as 'pond yachts'.

either case they provide insights into the history of model sailing which are not to be found in the more straightforward 'how to' books that make up the bulk of the field. To put the more substantial titles on 'serious' model yachting into their historical context, this bibliography also includes everything we have been able to find on practical sailing models, other than scale models of full size sailing craft.

Except in treating books which deal with both sail and power models, there is no coverage of powered models. However, there are a number of items which we have not been able to examine. With some of these, we cannot determine from their titles alone whether they contain material on sailing models. These items have been given the benefit of the doubt and included.

The commentary is, by the standards of most bibliographical writing, extensive. We make no apology for this; we envisage that our target audience will wish to use this book as a way of understanding what has been written about the sport over the years. They will need to know something about the contents of the fairly obscure titles that we deal with. Writing the commentary, particularly on the less satisfactory books, has been fun and we regard it as a recompense for the tedium involved in putting together as accurate a collection of bibliographical detail as possible.

Predecessors
There is no directly comparable earlier work, but two earlier bibliographies make some attempt to cover the field. Van Stockum[2] calls his book an attempt at a bibliography. Though it covers four languages, it is very limited in its time span. Even so, in respect of model yachting, and indeed full size yachting also, it is seriously deficient. Toy's bibliography of yachting[3] covers only English language publications, but its section on model yachting gives fairly comprehensive cover of those books whose titles clearly reveal their contents, including a sprinkling of texts on radio control. It is clear however from his brief comments that he has not seen many of them, or if he has, he has misunderstood them. He does mention a few titles that we might not have found elsewhere. Richard Cox's otherwise admirable *Sport in Britain*[4] contains no coverage of model sports.

---

2 Van STOCKUM, C M: *Sport: An Attempt at a Bibliography of Books and Periodicals. 1890-1912*: New York, Dodd and Livingston, 1914.
3 TOY, Ernest W: *Adventurers Afloat, a Bibliography of Yachting*: Metuchen, NJ and London, Scarecrow, 1988.
4 COX, Richard W: *Sport in Britain: A Bibliography of Historical Publications, 1800-1988*: Manchester, Manchester UP, 1991.

Organisation

The listing is organised in three sections, dealing in turn with books on model sailing craft, with material on the development of radio control and finally with the range of periodicals that have covered the sport over the years. Within sections the listings are alphabetical by author or title as appropriate. Where an author has more than one title to his name, they are entered in date order of first publication.

With only one exception, we have not included catalogues from commercial suppliers. Though some of these contain valuable information, it is extremely difficult to access a representative collection and even more difficult to know where to draw the line between the serious model engineering emporia and the long tail of producers of increasingly inadequate toys.

There is extensive cross-referencing between the entries and where an author or periodical is mentioned for which there is a separate entry, the name appears in **bold**. A number of the periodicals changed their names or went through a series of mergers with other titles. In each case, the main entry is under the **earliest** title, with other titles (where they are significantly different) given a separate entry referring the user to the main entry.

Primary Sources

We have included no treatment of primary sources. There are two reasons for this; as a result of losses over the years (and of extreme parsimony of effort by the administrators of clubs, national and international associations), they are extremely sparse. More important, we have found that they contain remarkably little of real value to a historian.

The Importance of Juvenile Literature

The most cursory inspection of the list of titles will reveal a high proportion, both of books and journals, that appear to be addressed to children rather than to adults. This first becomes apparent in the middle years of the 19th century. At this time there was a coincidence of more widespread education, producing a more or less completely literate society, with improvements in printing technology and, perhaps most important, in the distribution arrangements for magazines. This changed the economic bases of book and magazine production and resulted in a very large increase in the number of titles for both adults and juveniles.

Many of the magazines, collections and compendia aimed specifically at younger readers claimed to include scientific and practical articles as well as the adventure fiction that was their mainstay. This is often an empty, or almost empty, boast, perhaps included to assist in selling the magazine to parents and schoolmasters as suitable for their young charges. Where there is any significant and continuing technical and practical content, it seems to have been widely assumed that something about sailing models was a necessary part of such an enterprise.

Though the model sailing material in these titles is intended for the young, it is necessarily written by adults, most of whom appear to have had extensive practical experience of the sport. What they suggest as the right thing for boys to do almost always reflects what would have been their own practice, even to the extent of proposing methods requiring skills that would have been beyond all but a tiny minority of their readers.

Many of the boy's journals reached a much wider audience than the schoolboys for whom they were primarily intended. The senior forms of public schools were, by Victorian standards, young men and *The Captain* specifically called itself 'a magazine for boys and old boys', making its pitch for a peculiarly English form of retarded adolescence. *Boy's Own Paper* certainly attracted a significant adult readership. Its period as the journal of record for model yachtsmen, after the demise of *The Model Yachtsman and Canoeist*, firmly established it as a place where adult enthusiasts wrote for their fellows, and this continued as long as the magazine continued to carry modelling material.

Another important, if differently motivated, strand of juvenile writing arose from the incorporation of model yachting into the state and Party dominated sports organisations of Nazi Germany. During the early years of the second world war, when it must have looked as if the thousand year *Reich* would become a reality, there was an upsurge of books, magazines and designs, many of them specifically aimed at the junior model yachting activity conducted by the *Hitlerjugend*. Several of these publications also carry the imprimatur of the 'central model building instructional workshop of the *Kriegsmarine*', and reflect a concern to use model yachting as a way to inculcate maritime, patriotic and nationalist ideas in the young, alongside the practical skills of building and sailing.

This overt attempt to use the sport as a brainwashing device is not peculiar to totalitarian regimes; it can also be seen in some of the writing for boys that came out of British Victorian concern to establish the right attitudes to the Navy and to British maritime imperialism.

At about the same date as the Nazi party was seeking to incorporate model yachting into its totalitarian leisure system, America was growing concerned about the inadequacy of vocational training in its schools. The result was that in many local school systems a concerted effort was made to include 'Industrial Arts' training as part of the high school curriculum. Though this is quintessentially an element of the New Deal approach to improving the state of the nation, it had its beginnings in the early years of the century and continues, in a much reduced form, to the present.

The subjects offered in the 'Industrial Arts' and 'shop' courses varied widely. In some school districts they were extremely ambitious. Many schools seem to have offered a general 'shop' course which, to arouse the enthusiasm of the pupils, was centred round the construction and sailing of model boats. Most schemes were based on relatively simple models that could be built in school and raced in local regattas, often sponsored by the city newspaper, the local Chamber of Commerce or Rotary. When conducted at city-wide level, these regattas could involve several hundred entrants.

A number of the instructors involved produced handbooks aimed in part at their fellow professionals, in part at the students themselves, setting out how to go about it and including plans. Of these 'Industrial Arts' originated texts, **Cavileer** is an early example, **Pozzini and Phillips** a very late one. **Horst** is by far the most prolific of this group of authors.

Availability
Practically all the books recorded here are long out of print. Second hand copies are to be had from specialist maritime booksellers, but with increasing difficulty and at rapidly escalating prices as the vintage yachting movement stimulates demand. Some can be obtained by diligent application to the reserve stocks of local libraries and to the inter-library loans service. Some others are being brought back into circulation by the Curved Air Press and by the publishing activity of the USVMYG. Most, but not all, of the British titles can be found in the British Library and other copyright libraries, as can some of the foreign titles. The British Library's holdings are, however, far from complete as regards successive editions.

Sources
The main sources for this work, apart from our own collections, have been the British Library and the bibliographical series that it contains. We have been given essential help with foreign language titles by a number of collectors.

Omissions

It would nevertheless be foolish to claim that this is a complete coverage. There must be items that we have missed. In particular, the existence of flourishing model yachting activity in over thirty nations affiliated to the Model Yacht Racing Division of the International Sailing Federation suggests that there must be many small circulation journals and possibly instructional texts that we have not been able to find. This applies with special force to material produced in East European and East Asian languages. There must also surely be more than one 'how to do it' book in the French language, but neither we nor those we have consulted have been able to find them.

We have almost certainly not found everything that appeared in general crafts compendia, encyclopaedias and boy's journals. We have not been able even to start to examine the range of such publications originating outside the UK.

Similarly, it has not been possible in all cases to discover the forenames of authors.

Model Yachting as a Technological Sport

Model yachting with a formal organisation at a local club level has existed in Britain at least since the early years of the 19th century; the sailing of models by individuals is recorded in a few scattered biographical sources from the 18th century. Though it is very likely that the sailing of models existed earlier, we have not been able to find any record of it. Outside Britain, the evidence is less clear, but the existence of organised clubs in the USA by the 1850s and in several European countries by the 1880s suggests that a similar pattern of development was seen there also.

In the UK, recorded inter-club competition and regional organisation appear in the 1880s and national organisation in the early years of the 20th century. Elsewhere, they seem to have developed somewhat later.

Though occasional international competitions took place from as early as 1853, these were organised by individuals and were pretty informal. International competition in a 'modern' form has existed only since 1913 and a formal international controlling organisation since 1927. This has become a truly effective world-wide body only with the expansion of the sport occasioned by the advent of competitive radio controlled sailing from the early 1970s onwards.

The history of model yachting is, like that of any other vehicle based sport, primarily the history of a technical and technological development. The long term aim of the sport is the improvement of the design, construction and ultimately the performance of the vehicle. As in any other sport, competitive pressure drives the search for more effective technologies at a speed which is matched only by the pressures that drive defence research and development.

Though in full size sailing, one design, mass produced boats have become the backbone of the competitive scene, model yachting has retained an attachment to development classes. One design classes are the exception rather than the rule in model sailing. In development classes, designers and builders have considerable freedom, within the constraints of the relevant Rating Rule, to vary the design of hull and rig in the pursuit of improved performance. This continuing use of development classes, with their emphasis on progress in design and construction, is made much easier in the model by the relatively low cost and negligible danger of experiment.

It has also produced in many model yachtsmen a tradition of continuous tinkering with their boats. This translates, for designers, into an adventurous approach to technical innovation and experiment. For this reason, and because the technical requirements of unmanned sailing craft can be more demanding than those of full size, manned craft, model practice has in many cases been in advance of that of full size yachtsmen.

Most of the serious writing from within the sport has been concerned with new designs, new methods of construction and the most effective deployment of current theoretical understanding and available technology. The sequence of design development, as recorded in lines plans published by designers, in their writings about design, and in surviving models from the past, forms the central spine around which any history of the sport must be built. It is for this reason that the commentary on the individual titles emphasises their contribution to this design and technical history.

The wider history of model yachting, its place in the history of sport and leisure, the social background of its participants, the multiple contexts of their activity and the meanings that they ascribed to what they were doing, are all much harder to disentangle. They are scarcely to be found in instructional texts, and have to be mined from between the lines in periodicals, in the ephemera of race reports and correspondence.[5]

---

5 A particularly cherishable example is found in a report of an inter-club race on Merseyside in 1912, at the height of the Home Rule crisis. Among the conventional boat names like *Spindrift, Bluebelle* and *Molly,* the North Liverpool club fielded a team of three boats named *Carson, Bonar Law* and *Red Hand.* It has not been possible to establish a link to the local Unionist organisations.

Radio Developments

Radio equipment with the potential to control models has been available since the early years of the 20th century. Tesla's original radio control patents in the 1890s were for the control of a small torpedo and much of the serious work on radio control before and during the First World War was directed to the production of radio controlled weapons, both sea and airborne. Radio controlled power models were seen before 1914 and isolated experiments with the control of sailing craft began in the 1930s, accelerating after 1945. Only in the late 1960s did the equipment become both sufficiently cheap and reliable to be used by model sailors without radio expertise, rather than being the preserve of radio experimenters who used sailing craft as safe and slow moving development vehicles. Reductions in the size and weight of equipment also allowed it to be applied to all sizes of model, instead of only to the very largest classes.

This brought important changes to the sport by stimulating an explosive growth in participation, particularly in those countries which had had little or no preceding free sailing activity. In turn, it has led to the development of a truly world-wide arena of international competition and to extreme competitive pressure on designers and skippers alike. Equally important, radio racing has changed the forms of competition, and with them the design features needed for success.

We have therefore included in a separate section many of the books which record the development of what has proved to be a critical technology. The very small number of books that deal specifically with the use of radio control in model yachts are included in the section of books on model yachting itself. There is a fuller discussion of the background to radio control literature in the introduction to the radio section.

Periodicals

The periodical materials are crucial to the history of the sport, and supply much that is lacking from the primary sources. Material on model yachting is not only found in the few magazines that have been specifically devoted to the sport. There is also valuable matter in general model magazines, in magazines covering a wide range of crafts and pastimes, and in titles concerned primarily with full size sailing. These sources are discussed in more detail in the introduction to the periodicals listing.

Artefacts

Though most of the literature is devoted to the construction and design of models, it would not be possible to write an effective account of their development without access to a large number of surviving examples of older styles of model yacht. Unlike full size sailing craft, models that have been retired from racing are seldom converted to other uses, so that, if they survive, they usually do so in something close to their original form.

Some models survive in sailing condition from the 1880s onwards, and the numbers increase as we approach the present, or at least until the early 1960s. At about this time, the typical construction of a competitive boat changed from wood to fibre reinforced plastic. Thus models became relatively cheaper and easier to throw away when their performance ceased to be competitive; at the same time they were less attractive as a piece of craftsmanship to the non-expert antique dealer or interior decorator.

The importance of surviving models is as evidence of the design practice of the past and of how boats were built, of how successful our predecessors were in their search for weight-efficient construction and, often, how their actual practice differed from the methods they prescribed in writing about construction.

Other artefacts can also provide important insights. A box of masts and spars which had obviously been a club's common 'discard box', allows us to reach conclusions about the classes sailed, and to observe the wide spread of construction practice and standards within a single club. Similarly, old sails, rescued from duty as clubhouse dusters, suggest that at the turn of the century the London MYC sailed boats even bigger than those recorded in their extensive measurement books. They also provide evidence of the superlatively high levels of sail construction and finish in the boats built for this very gentlemanly club.

The examination, reconstruction and operation of old boats is central to the study of the technical history of model yachting and is a large part of the *raison d'être* of the Vintage Model Yacht Group, which was founded in 1987. Restored boats can be operated and their performance studied. Only by racing boats to the same Rule but from different periods, over an extended series of trials, can improvement be quantified. This is only rarely possible, but critical examination of the performance of older boats, even when sailed alone, can give considerable insight into what they are capable of and a sense of the rate of advance in performance.

Apart from the use of old boats as evidence for the history of the sport, many of them are objects of great beauty. This can only enhance the pleasure derived from the engineering and performance of that supremely elegant machine, the sailing boat.

Acknowledgements

We are grateful for the assistance of a number of people who have supplied information or have helped in other ways.

Roger Bridgman and Henry Farley helped us avoid error in our treatment of radio developments; Richard W Cox gave advice on the niceties of bibliographical practice; Chris Jackson and Jean-Pierre Dole Robbe assisted with information on French language periodicals. Gerd Menkens went far beyond the call of duty in supplying details, and often copies, of many German and other European titles and in closely supervising our transcription of the languages with which we were not familiar. Graham Reeves supplied information on the long discontinued **MYA News**. Earl Boebert, Don Kihlstrom and Charley Williamson, members of the USVMYG, all helped us with some of the American titles. Juan Roig has placed us in his debt by finding, copying and having bound for us a copy of **Carulli**'s book of 1946. Gregg K. Dietrich of North Star Galleries, New York, put us on to a title in the antiques sphere that we would otherwise have missed. Ghillian Potts has been a conscientious proof reader and stylistic adviser.

Needless to say, any remaining errors and omissions are ours; we shall be pleased to receive corrections and additions for a future edition.

Russell Potts
Paul Croxson

BOOKS ON SAILING MODELS

The records of the earliest sailing activity are all retrospective; there are no contemporary printed sources from before the middle of the 19th century. What we have takes the form of memories of childhood and early youth recalled in extreme old age and retailed in letters to journals.

The steady trickle of book titles wholly devoted to model yachting does not begin until the late 1870s, followed in the mid 1880s by the first journal devoted exclusively to the sport. After this date there is an almost continuous sequence of periodicals that attempt to fill the role of a journal of record.

Most books on model yachting have been 'how to do it' texts, instructing the reader in the building, equipping and sailing of models. They vary widely in their sophistication; some are superficial in the extreme; they are included for the sake of completeness and for the light they throw on the context within which the more serious writers were working. For the benefit of those seeking reliable information on the practice of seriously competitive skippers over the years, we have marked with an asterisk (*) those titles that were, in their generation, the leading texts, written by leading practitioners.

Some of these more solid titles give space to design concepts and procedures; in this they bear comparison with the parallel stream of writings on the design of full size sailing craft, much of which is directed to the gentleman amateur yacht owner, rather than to the professional. All the 'how to do it' titles contain substantial numbers of illustrations. Almost all contain at least some designs from which the reader might build himself a boat. These again are noted in the commentary.

1   ADAM, Harvey A: *Model Boat Construction*:
London, Percival Marshall, 1952: xvii, 102, oblong
folio.

This large format, well produced book is mainly concerned with
ambitious scale and semi-scale powered models of motor torpedo
boats and the like, but does contain two projects for sailing vessels.
The author writes from a background in engineering, buttressed by
serious wealth. He is clearly never troubled by the need for
economy in any of his modelling projects; the sails for his very
small dinghy models were made up specially for him by Ratsey and
Lapthorn, the Cowes sailmakers.

In his power boats, Adam operated at the cutting edge of the
available technology. He describes various forms of clockwork and
electric powered cam operated steering devices, as well as a radio
control system that he used in his larger powered models. This
used an imported American tuned reed system, with which he had
made some impressive long distance runs in the Solent. He claims
to have been planning an attempt on the Channel crossing, but it is
not clear whether this was ever made, or whether he was
anticipated by George Honnest Redlich's 1951 crossing. (See No.
166)

Both the sailing models are for dinghies. One is a 16 inch
sharpie. The other is a more ambitious 18 inch dinghy, to be clinker
planked in $1/32$ inch waterproof ply over frames and a built up
backbone. The latter design was briefly available in the late 1940s
(before the publication of the book) as an expensive kit under the
'Adamcraft' label, as were some of the power boats.[6]

2   ANON: *Your Model Yacht, How to Sail it; Practical
Hints for the Young Novice*: **by a Member of one of
the Leading Model Yacht Clubs: London, The
Model Yachtsman, n.d. (1929?): 12, 8°.
2nd edition: London, The Curved Air Press,
(VMYG Reprint No.1): 1990:
ISBN 1 873148 00 3: 12, 21cm.**

This is a very simple pamphlet, aimed at schoolboys. It deals with
techniques for sailing the simplest types of models, with no
steering gear, or with weighted rudders.

---

[6] The kit, though ambitiously produced and advanced in its conception, was
   something less than a perfected example of production engineering. I
   failed to build one successfully as a boy of 14, and I am having almost
   as much difficulty with another example fifty years later. **RP.**

For all that, it is clear and comprehensive and in its reprint edition has enabled collectors of vintage models who do not have model yachting experience to display their treasures on the water in a competent manner.

3   BASSETT-LOWKE: *How to Sail Your Model Yacht*:
         London, Bassett-Lowke, n. d. (1950s): 12, 8º.
         2nd edition: London, The Curved Air Press,
         (VMYG Reprint No.2) 1990: ISBN 1 873148 01 1:
         12, 21cm.

This pamphlet must originally have been intended to accompany the very superior toy boats sold by this most superior of model engineering emporia. It is aimed at fond uncles and their favourite nephews and deals clearly with basic sailing techniques, including the use of the Braine automatic steering gear.

The copy from which the CAP edition has been reproduced dates from the 1950s, but the text was almost certainly written originally in the 1930s.

*4   BAUDUIN, F: *Het Ontwerpen, Vervaardigen en
         Zeilen van Model-Zeiljachten: Zaandam, Blees,
         1925: 158, 8º.*

This work is written by a retired Engineer Admiral of the RNN. We have seen only part of this text, the only Dutch originated title that we have been able to discover.

Bauduin gives considerable space to a vane steering device of his own design, first published in a Dutch journal *Ons Element.* As a result he entered into a correspondence with H Hambley Tregonning, a British model yachtsman, who had developed a similar vane gear, which is also depicted. When Tregonning first demonstrated his vane to fellow members of the MYSA, he was shown extensive correspondence that Bauduin had had with George Braine. It is clear that Bauduin was a close follower of British practice.

Both the steering gears are masthead vanes in the style of those used by Herreshoff, originally in the 1870s. They are pretty crude in execution and seem innocent of any balancing of the large and fairly heavy vane components. Bauduin does give some thought to the problem of weight and gravity, but does not really have an answer, other than suggesting that in some situations, the weight of the vane components can be an advantage.

It seems unlikely that either can have been very effective, despite Bauduin's assertion that Tregonning had enjoyed the advantage of developing his gear in the highly competitive environment of London model yacht clubs. Though Bauduin attaches some importance to Tregonning's work, there is only the barest trace of it in the British model journals of the time, apart from a brief article on its application to a non class boat that appeared in **Boys' Own Paper** in 1924. In the mid thirties, when Scandinavian styles of vane gear were becoming known in Britain, there are suggestions that races had been won on the Round Pond with vane equipped boats, but these are not specifically attributed to Tregonning, and no contemporary record of such victories has been found.

Much of the rest of the book is given over to retailing to his Dutch readership the state of the game in the UK and Germany, as depicted in the 1913 and subsequent editions of **Marshall's** *Model Sailing Yachts* and in **Tiller's** *Modellyachtbau*. There are reproductions of plans from both sources including Daniels' 10-rater *Electra*; much of the expository material on design procedure and calculation is based on Daniels' designs.

*5   BIDDLE, Tyrrel E: *Model Yacht Building and Sailing: A Treatise on the Construction, Rigging and Handling of Model Yachts, Ships and Steamers, with Remarks on Cruising and Racing Yachts and on the Handling of Open Boats:* London, Charles Wilson, 1879: 107, 8°.
2nd, 'enlarged' edition: London, Imray, Laurie, Norie and Wilson, 1883: 117, 8°.

This is the first 'how to do it' book and contains comprehensive instructions on the building and rigging of model sailing craft in the style of the period.

Biddle was one of a family of four brothers. Three of them served as merchant marine officers under sail and at least two were active model yachtsmen in London from the 1850s. T E himself was a member of the club on the Serpentine in the 1850s, and a founder member of clubs at Clapham in 1863, Victoria Park in the middle sixties and of the Model Yacht Sailing Association (MYSA) at Kensington in 1876. He was also an active yachtsman and wrote introductory volumes on yachting and on yacht design. His brother R F, always referred to as 'Captain', spent his retirement as a minor marine artist and at the time of his death in 1885 was Treasurer of the MYSA.

As the title suggests, the contents are not confined to model yachting; some of the text is devoted to topics reflecting the author's wide range of maritime interests and his background as a merchant service officer.

The second edition is described as 'enlarged', but contains only slight additional matter on the organisation of a model yacht club and on the sailing Rules. These almost certainly reflect the contemporary practice of the MYSA. In the introduction to this edition, Biddle complains of plagiarism by another author. Neither of the two works that appeared between the two editions of this work (**WALTON**, No. 150 and **GROSVENOR**, No. 54) is, in our view, in any way similar to Biddle's book. Unless there was quite another book that has since been lost from sight, Biddle was being oversensitive. In his articles in *Boys' Own Paper* he speaks approvingly of Walton's book, so it is unlikely that he regarded him as the culprit.

The text covers design considerations and the procedures of drawing up a design, together with comprehensive instructions for the construction and rigging of a model. The preferred method of hull construction is carving from bread and butter lifts, which he regards as superior to plank-on-frame methods for the relatively small size of hull with which he is concerned. There is treatment of more unusual construction methods from tin or zinc plate, but these also Biddle does not favour.

The first edition contains the lines for a full size yacht to the then current YRA Rule (the '94' Tonnage Rule). In the second edition this is replaced by a 10 Tonner to the new YRA Rule (the '1730' Tonnage Rule of 1881). On the model side, the first edition has lines for a two foot model cutter and the second adds drawings for a 36 inch waterline cutter to the Rule used by the Victoria Park club and for a 30 inch waterline yawl to the MYSA Rule.

Other plates include drawings of a cutter rig for a model that appear to have been prepared for this work, as well as fairly standard engravings of the standing and running rigging of a square rigged ship. These last are the sort of blocks that his nautical specialist publishers would almost certainly have in stock and would have used in other titles. There are however a large number of small engravings of model fittings and construction details in the text that seem to have been made specially for this work.

*6   BLACK, John: *Yachting with Models*: New York
         and London, McGraw Hill, (Whittlesey House),
         1939: xvi, 293, 8°.
This book by a leading American model yachtsman of the 1930s deserves to be better known than it is in Britain. Its publication on the eve of the Second World War no doubt contributed to its lack of impact. Black was a crafts teacher in schools in the Boston area and a member of clubs in Boston, Marblehead and elsewhere in the

North Eastern states. He had roots in Scotland and was a frequent visitor to the UK.

He was one of the group of East Coast modellers who were instrumental in founding the Model Yacht Racing Association of America (MYRAA) in the early 1920s, initially as a vehicle for channelling the US challenges for the *Yachting Monthly* Cup; he was also active in the International Model Yacht Racing Association which was founded in 1927. By the time he wrote his book he was President of IMYRA, as well as an office holder in MYRAA.

He himself sailed for the *Yachting Monthly* Cup on a number of occasions, coming within a single point of victory in 1927. In 1936 he won international races for the Marblehead class held in Hamburg in association with the Berlin Olympics of that year.

His book is concerned almost entirely with the Marblehead class. It is telling evidence of the impact of this smaller and simpler class of model on the American model yachting scene that Black, who had designed and built the famous *Bostonia* series of 'A' Class boats for his *Yachting Monthly* Cup campaigns, makes no mention of them. There is careful treatment of construction by both bread and butter and plank-on-frame methods, together with material on fittings, sail making and rigging. Appendices give details of the 'M' Class Rule, the MYRAA Sailing Rules, and addresses of model yacht clubs and suppliers in the US.

Surprisingly, given Black's undoubted ability in the field, there is no discussion of design considerations. He gives the lines of two of his Marblehead designs, *Cheerio*, the winning boat in Hamburg, and *Cheerio II*, which was then his latest design. These are unfortunately to a small and indeterminate scale.

There is valuable information on the introduction of the vane steering gear into US practice in the late 1930s, and of the attitudes of some skippers to what they saw as increasing 'mechanisation' of model sailing. He is aware of experiments with radio control and envisages a time when the sport will have to decide whether it is to be admitted into competitive sailing.

The implication of his discussion is that he would have been among those agin it, but he does not discuss in detail what his objection would have been. It is fairly clear that, like **Daniels and Tucker** somewhat later (No. 33), he did not envisage the development of fleet racing under radio control.

7   BLANDFORD, Percy William: *Model Boat Construction*: London, Foyle's, 1954: 96, 8º. Another edition, London, Frederick Muller, 1954, 96, 8º.

Reprinted, Frederick Muller, 1955: 96, 8º.

Reprinted, Leamington Spa, TEE Publishing, (Past Masters) 1994.

A generalised description of construction techniques for both sail and power models, this title contains no plans. There is a chapter on the design considerations for sailing models and one on their fitting and rigging, which contains a treatment of the Braine gear. Despite the date, there is no mention of vane gears, nor of sailcloth other than cotton. Though the treatment is brief, it is quite comprehensive and encapsulates late 1930s practice, with little concession to the technical and materials developments that were beginning to affect competitive sailing by the time it appeared.

The relationship between the two versions is not clear. Apart from the title pages they are identical and appear to have been published in parallel by Foyle's and by Muller; possibly Muller had originated the title and it was then taken into the Foyle's series. Most, but not all, of the other Foyle's handbook titles appear only under their own imprint.

*8   BORN, Karl Peter: *RC Yachtsegeln Theorie und Praxis für den RC-Jachtsegelsport (Modell Fachbuch)*: Villingen-Schwenningen, Neckar-Verlag, 2nd edition, 1985: 64, 24 cm.

We have not seen this, which appears to be a treatment of modern competitive sailing. We have not been able to discover the date of the first edition.

*9   BOWDEN, Claude Evelyn: *Model Yacht*
Construction & Sailing: the Principles of the
Design, Construction and Operation of Model and
Small Racing Craft in the Light of Modern
Knowledge of Aerodynamics and Hydrodynamics:
London, Percival Marshall, 1946: 93, 8º.
2nd Revised edition, 1949: 104, 8º.

US edition, New York, 1950.

3rd Revised edition, 1952: 137, 8º.

4th Enlarged and Revised edition, 1956.

Reprint of 1952 edition, Leamington Spa, TEE
Publishing, (Past Masters), 1994.

Claude Bowden was a pioneer aeromodeller and in the 1930s did
much to develop practical petrol engined flying models. He was a
mechanical engineer and his expertise was in the design and
construction of small internal combustion engines. His skills as a
designer and builder of aircraft were not exceptional.

At the end of the war in 1945 he was in Germany with the
army and, through the R&R sailing of yachts requisitioned from
the German armed forces, became interested in the problems of
sailing and in German practice in the design and sailing of
dinghies and small keel boats. This was in many respects in
advance of and more 'scientific' than comparable British activity
and was conveniently described in Curry's writings of the 1920s.

This book seeks to apply these insights systematically to
model design and sailing. There are no lines plans, but much
information on his experiments with planing hulls, wing sails,
through battened sails and (in the later editions) early radio
control and the use of glass reinforced plastic as a constructional
material. These experiments were conducted entirely outside the
orbit of the Model Yachting Association, partly because the Rating
Rules prohibited many of the concepts he wanted to explore, partly
because he had had a falling out with the old guard of the
Association.

The ingenuity of his ideas, many of which were at variance
with the received wisdom, was not matched by his construction
techniques, which were crude and, given his background in
aeromodelling, surprisingly unconscious of the need for weight
control. Our examination and sailing of one of his models long after
his death made clear that he was often unable to reap the full

rewards of his advanced concepts because his physical execution of them was inadequate.

As he seems never to have participated in mainstream competition, his work had little impact at the time. He was best known among model yachtsmen for his extended polemic with H B Tucker over the applicability of his concepts to model yachting. He can be seen, with the benefit of hindsight and more sophisticated production engineering, to have been right on almost every point.

The fourth edition, which we have not seen, appears to contain some further additional matter.

The book contains some interesting material on, and photos of John Alexander, a noted commercial builder of the period, at work on a 6-metre for Bowden, demonstrating the builder's preferred technique of building by bread and butter on the buttocks.

10   BOYD, Norman: *The Discovery of Ship Models*:
Colchester, Napier, 1983: ISBN: 0 946235 01 5: 153,
21 cm.

This work is devoted almost entirely to static models, considered as works of art and craftsmanship. It ranges from votive models through Navy Board models to modern plastic kits. There are a couple of paragraphs on practical sailing models, which suggest that the author has little knowledge of them.

This title has escaped the British Library and all the usual bibliographical sources. Despite a claim on the reverse title that it is first published in 1983 by Napier, there was an earlier, much slighter work under the same title, published in paperback by Shire Press in 1971. We have seen only the 1983 edition.

11   BOYS' OWN: *Model Yachts, Sailing Boats and
Submarines*: London, BOP (Religious Text
Society) ("How to Make" Books), 1924: 190, 8º.

This is a collection of articles that appeared originally in *BOP*, some dating from as far back as the 1890s. About half the contributions deal with sailing models. They make up a very mixed bag, ranging from what was, in its time, state of the art practice in serious competition, to descriptions of crude home built toys. The more weighty articles include designs for early 10-raters originating in the Clapham club and another 10-r of the 1890s by McClachlan.

The Clapham article is by W J Gordon, a *BOP* regular and author of popular works on railways. It throws valuable light on attitudes to design developments and to the Rating Rules of the time, as well as the problems of middle class amateurs in finding the right materials to build their boats.

12   **BREMNER, David: 'Shipbuilding', in** *Cassell's Book of Sports and Pastimes*: **London, Cassell, 1881: xii, 975, 8°.**

2nd edition, 1886.

3rd edition, 1892 (also in 1892 as *Cassell's Complete Book of Sports and Pastimes*).

4th edition, 1896; 5th edition, 1903.

6th edition, 1907.

This is a thirteen page article in a large compendium. It is typical of the material offered in non-specialist magazines and compendia of the period, not least in the material surrounding the actual instructions on building. This paints a romantic vision of the joys of seeing one's creation 'ploughing her way through a ripple' and recommends model sailing as a way of 'driving out any half formed notion of running away to sea' that might trouble young men.

> In teaching our pupil how to build and sail a model yacht we are therefore providing him with a means of healthy recreation that will not necessarily unsettle his mind or create in him a desire to roam.

The care taken to reassure mama that young master Willy will not be unsettled is touching.

The instructions for carving a 24 inch cutter hull from the solid are much abbreviated; there are no lines plans and little information on how the desired shape is to be achieved. After dealing with carving from the solid, Bremner remarks that this is a primitive method, suggestive 'of the practice of a savage people' and proposes a planked model from '⅛ inch planks of fine grained mahogany'. He does not however suggest how such a planked model might be built.

On the other hand there are passing and unexplained references to design concepts, such as optimum length to beam ratios and the need for the delivery to be matched to the entry. These suggest that Bremner's original text was longer and was arbitrarily reduced by his editor, and that he could have written something more serious had he had more space.

Though he emphasises the need to keep the weight of spars and top hamper to a minimum, the details of the rig he suggests closely follow full size practice, with fidded topmast, superfluous shrouds and overlapping head sails.

The article ends with a brief treatment of the building of a schooner of unspecified size.

The later editions of the compendium are more cheaply produced and less fully illustrated, with much of the contents re-written in a simpler form. The workshop section, including the 'Shipbuilding' article appears to be the only part that is unchanged in the later editions.

13   **BRINTON, J:** *Model Yacht Sailing for Competition and Pleasure*: **London, British Sports Publishing (Spalding's Athletic Library, No 15), 1928: 22, 8⁰.**

A very short, unsophisticated treatment, which bears little relation to what competitive model yachtsmen were doing at the period. It is chiefly valuable as evidence that Spalding's sold a range of model boats as part of their large sporting goods business. Brinton is noted in the British Library catalogue as, 'of the Isle of Wight', and may have been the craftsman who provided Spalding's with their models. There are photos of some small models but no drawings and no worthwhile building instructions.

*14   **BROWNE, Denis R H:** *Model Sailing Yachts*: **London, Robert Ross/Harrap, 1950: 124, 8⁰.**

This book, written by an engineer and full size yachtsman who was a member of the YM6 Owners Association, offers a thorough coverage of the immediate post war scene. The emphasis is almost entirely on the 'A' Class and the text deals with hull design considerations and the aerodynamics of sails, as well as sail trimming and sailing techniques, including the use of both Braine and vane steering gears. There is also some discussion of the speeds that could be reached by model yachts.

Interestingly there is no constructional information. This is a book for upper middle class owners who, like the owners of full size yachts, might design their boat and would certainly sail it, but who would expect to employ a craftsman to actually build it.

Browne is much influenced by the design practice of Howard Nash, another engineer and YM6 member who was one of the leading 'A' Class designers and skippers of the period. There is detailed coverage of the 1948 'All Nations' race at Gosport and of the 1949 competition at Fleetwood, in which *Ranger* won the *Yachting Monthly* Cup for America for the first time.

There is extended discussion of the then current styles of design in the 'A' Class and the lines of two important boats are included, *Fantasy III* by Howard Nash and *Revanche* by the Dane, Kai Ipsen.

15   BRUYCKER, Adolf de: *Drei schnelle Modell-Renn-yachten, 'Racker', 'Rüpel' und 'Lümmel', der Jugendklassen G und F und der Klasse E der Modellsegelabteilung des DSV im NSRL. Beschreibung des spantlosen Bauverfahrens*: Berlin, Delius, Klasing, 1941: 19, 4º.

This slight pamphlet was meant to accompany full size plan sets for each of the models discussed. These were sold separately for 60 Pf, 90 Pf and 1 Mark 60 respectively.

We have not seen the whole of the text but it contains a drawing of a vane gear that is right up to date for its period and clearly influenced by the latest US practice. As in his later works, de Bruycker is proposing his frameless construction around a shaped block.

This *spantloser* (frameless) building technique is unusual; all three designs are to be built round a shaped block rather than on bulkheads or shadows. The claimed advantage is weight reduction, particularly important in a small class such as this. As de Bruycker was a school teacher, it is possible that this is a technique that was evolved to permit 'mass production' of a one design boat by a school class. Other plans by de Bruyker for boats on this system exist.

The long title makes clear that at this date, as now, model sailing was fully integrated into the German national authority for full size sailing and that both, in 1941, were incorporated into the Nazi Party structure for the organisation of sport and leisure activity. The title page of the copy we have seen also includes a rubric indicating the approval of the *Lehrwerkstatt der Kriegsmarine für Schiffmodellbau* (the German Navy Ship Model Training Workshop).

*16   BRUYCKER, Adolf de: *Klassen-und Regattabestimmungen (Modell-Segeln Series No 1)*: Wolfenbuttel, Kallmeyer, 1956: 48, 8º.

We have not seen this title. It appears to be a treatment of the Rating and Racing rules for model yachts.

*17   BRUYCKER, Adolf de: *Modellsegeln; der Bau spantloser Modellyachten: (Modell-Segeln Series No 2)*: Wolfenbuttel, Kallmeyer, 1956: 48, 8º.

This is another brief treatment of building techniques, centred round three different designs to the *Deutscher Seglerverband* Class G. There are no plans as such; presumably they were available separately, as with those discussed at No. 16. Class G was a junior class with a range of maximum and minimum dimensions. The length had to be between 650 and 750 mm. and the sail area not more than 0.21 square metres.

The three designs are: a very simple flat bottomed sharpie, a slightly more sophisticated V-bottom sharpie and a round bottom, planked hull. This last envisages the use of a sophisticated triple diagonal planking system, while the sharpies were to be built in either 1 mm. or 1.5 mm. ply.

The rig is the same for all three hulls, a simple bermuda sloop. There is no mention of steering gear in the sailing instructions and no rudder is mentioned in the comprehensive parts list, so we must assume that these designs were simplified for use by schoolchildren. Other designs to this class from the 1930s, e.g. those in Tiller (No. 137) have practicable rudders and automatic steering gears.

18   **BULLIVANT, Cecil H: *Every Boy's Book of Hobbies*: London and Edinburgh, TC and EC Jack, 1912: 534, 8⁰.**

The model boat element in this large and wide ranging book is only a few pages. Chapter 12 discusses ways of waterproofing simple boats made in paper, using animal glues treated with bichromate of potash. This method was still advocated by **Reeves** (No. 118) forty years later. The chapter on model sailing boats is almost entirely given over to a 'windmill boat', to be propelled by a mast-mounted windmill driving a water screw through two sets of bevel gearing. Though sound in principle, it is unlikely that the mechanism proposed would be able to overcome its own in-built friction.

| 19 | CAMM, Frederick James: *Model Boat Building*: (Newnes' Home Mechanics Series): London, Newnes, 1940: 144, 8°. |
| | Reprinted, 1942. |

US edition, New York, Chemical Publishing, 1940.

4th edition, London, Newnes, 1946: 144, 8°.

5th edition, London, Newnes, 1948.

6th edition, London, Newnes, 1948.

Reprinted, Leamington Spa, TEE Publishing, (Past Masters) 1994.

Camm wrote prolifically on a wide range of popular technical subjects in the inter war years, particularly on internal combustion engines for model aircraft and boats, and on home built wireless and television. He was brother to Sidney Camm the aircraft designer and had been an active aeromodeller from before 1914. His main modelling activity in the inter war years seems to have been in power boats.

This is a slight and slipshod work, and was seriously out of date even on its first publication. The treatment of the Rating Rules is riddled with unnoticed misprints and suggests an unwillingness to do his homework on material outside his normal field. The plans are all for non-class boats and the approach is, in general, crude. Camm has individual ideas on how the Rating Rules should be drawn.

The British Library holds only the 1940 edition. Advertisements for the 5th edition, which we have not seen, suggest that there is some new material, but a comparison of the 6th edition with the first shows them to be identical. (See also No. 102).

*20   CARULLI, Arnoldo Bartolomé: *Diseño, Construcción y Navegación de Yates Modelos (Collección Pan America, Vol I)*: Buenos Aires, Klug Marchino, 1946: 174, 4°.
The copy we have seen has no publication date, but a printers' date of September 1948.

This is the only book on model yachting in Spanish that we or our informants have been able to discover. It is further evidence of a continuing model sailing activity in Argentina that dates back to before 1914 (See the entry on **HOBBS,** *Model Sailing Boats* (No. 66).

It is a competent and serious work and shows a close familiarity with the literature of British and US practice up to about 1939. Its treatment of the design process is extensive and discusses both volumetric balance in the style of Daniels and Turner's metacentric shelf concepts.

Construction proposals include carving from the solid, bread and butter on both waterlines and on the buttocks, and a good treatment of plank-on-frame methods, though nothing that had not appeared elsewhere. The chapter on steering gears treats weighted rudders, Braine gear and vanes of the Berge type, but does not pick up US practice of the late 1930s and 1940s. The section on sailmaking is, as is nearly always the case, brief and some way short of being an effective guide to how to do it, but the deficiency is in the description rather than in the expertise.

There is a section discussing the requirements for a model yacht lake, and one giving details of the Racing Rules and of a range of rating Rules. These are the Marblehead, the 10-rater and the American B Class, together with a local one metre class with restrictions on beam and draft and a maximum sail area of 5,000 cm². The design offered, with full size plans, is for a boat to this class, the *Gallareta.* Construction is to be by bread and butter and a ballast ratio of 67% is expected. The design is credited to CAYM, rather than to an individual.

21   CAPITMAN, William: *Sailing Small Boats*: New York, Padell Book Co., 1955.
We have not seen this. It may not be a model book at all.

22   CASSELL: *Cassell's Household Guide to Every Department of Practical Life, being a Complete Encyclopaedia of Domestic and Social Economy*: London, Cassell, Petter, Galpin & Co., 1869-70: 4 volumes, 4°.
Re-issued, 1873-4.
New and revised edition, 1881-3.
re-issued 1884.

We have seen only the relevant extract from this work, which was almost certainly issued originally in weekly parts.

Vol 4 of the 'new and revised' edition of 1881 contains, under the rubric 'Household Amusements XXXIII - Model Ship Building' a multi part article on the construction of a model of a 45 foot, 25 Ton cutter rigged yacht. This is at a scale of ³⁄₄ inch to the foot to give a model with a hull length of about 34 inches. The design and plank-on-frame construction proposed are close to full size practice, with much attention given to fittings and deck arrangements. There is nothing in the drawings or text that is inconsistent with this material having appeared in the first edition of 1869-71.

The author remarks that 'the lines of a vessel suitable for a model and the proper mode of constructing it have hitherto been almost unattainable', and recommends his model and method as likely 'to prevent further waste of time and annoyance, that must ever attend the making of unshapeable models as are usually met with'.

The drawings are small, but supplemented by a table of offsets and a number of constructional details that show that the author expected his readers, whom he envisaged as schoolboys, to reproduce much of the complex carpentry of full size practice. The author is clearly a full size shipbuilder and simply scales down normal yacht building practice wherever possible. Dimensions throughout are given in full size terms, producing disconcerting references to 'the side planks, two inches in thickness', though these are to be 'fixed with $1/4$ inch fine cut brads'.

Given that it is a scale model of a yacht, rather than a model yacht in the modern sense, this is a very competent piece of work, and the author clearly knew what he was about. He probably misjudged the abilities of his readers, few of whom would have been able to produce the levels of skill needed to complete the model in the way he describes.

23   CAVILEER, John W: *Model Boat Building for Boys*: Milwaukee WI, Bruce Publishing, 1923: 72, 4⁰.

Cavileer was a teacher in a Junior High School in Montclair NJ and his book covers the usual tools, materials and methods and deals with power models as well as sail.

There are three sail designs; for 24 and 30 inch sharpies and for a 36 inch round bottom boat. They appear not to be to any of the then current US model classes and the drawings show a rather old fashioned cutter rig for the largest of the three. There is mention of Marconi rig in the text, but among the very large number of very varied models that are shown in the illustrations, there is only one that appears to use this style. The steering gears offered are weighted rudders and a simple reverse tiller gear.

Cavileer ran a boat building programme in the school, or possibly as an extra-curricular activity, and over 100 boys from the 7th and 8th grades competed in a regatta. The clothes shown in the photographs reinforce the impression given by the designs he offers that Cavileer was writing about activities that had taken place some years before his book was published.

24   CHAPMAN, Charles: *A Book for Boys All About Ships, Showing the Way In the Hawsehole and Out of the Cabin Window, With the Way to Make Model Ships, etc.*: London, Edward Colyer, 1867: 32, 8°. Originally published as 12 separate short parts, of which this is only one.

New edition, first collected in one printing: 2 parts, (the second part is a glossary of maritime terms): London, Colyer, 1869.

New edition, 2 parts, London, Simpkin Marshall, 1873.

The model building section is very brief, scarcely more than a page and a half, but obviously written by someone with practical experience. He makes it clear that models need to be of different proportions from full size craft and suggests practical ways of going about most tasks, but necessarily very abbreviated. There are no usable plans.

25   CHICAGO PARKS DISTRICT: *Miniature Sailboats*: Chicago, Chicago Parks District, 1940: 24, folio, cyclostyled from typescript.

We have not seen this. The Chicago Park administrations took their responsibility to the citizens seriously. Before 1934, when the Parks District was formed by the amalgamation of the separate boards for each of the major parks in the city, the South Park Board had produced a number of pamphlets on things to do in the park, including titles on aircraft modelling.

After amalgamation, the new city-wide administration became the channel through which New Deal funds from the federal Works Progress Administration flowed to provide an amazingly wide range of leisure activities. These were intended to offer wholesome activity for the unemployed and work for those hired as organisers. The WPA also funded major expenditure on permanent facilities. The model yacht pond at Berkeley and the current clubhouse of the San Francisco club are among their projects. Chicago got a new model yacht pond at this period, but we have not seen any mention of WPA involvement with this.

Out of this activity in Chicago came a flood of short cyclostyled pamphlets on an amazing range of sports, games, crafts, amateur dramatics and many other topics. No individual authors are credited; most are simply 'by the Crafts Department'.

Even the plays about the history of Chicago, specially written for amateur performance, are 'by the Writers Program of the WPA, with the co-operation of the Chicago Parks District'. The whole programme offers an interesting sidelight on the only moment when the history of the USA briefly took a collective turn.

It took them a while to get round to model sailboats, which appears to be one of the last of their publications in this vein.

We know about this activity because the Chicago administration took care that their work was lodged in a number of libraries and thus is recorded in the *National Union Catalog* and the New York Public Library *Guide to Research Collections*. Other cities may have been equally enterprising, but failed to ensure that their work was preserved for posterity.

26   **CHILDS, Thomas H: *Model Sailing Vessels*: 1929.**
We have not seen this and can offer no bibliographical detail.

27   ***CHILDRENS' BRITANNICA*: Auckland, London,**
          Britannica, 1988.
The entry on 'Model-making' is brief and most of it is given over to aeromodelling. Within the boat modelling element, power is favoured over sail, but the very small amount that there is on model yachting is accurate and sensible.

*28   **CLAUGHTON, Andrew, Ian HOWLETT and Roger**
          STOLLERY: 'An Assessment of the Progress in
          Model Yacht Design through an Examination of
          Model Yacht Characteristics', in *Proceedings of*
          ***the Eighth Chesapeake Sailing Yacht Symposium*:**
          Baltimore MD, Chesapeake Yacht Racing
          Association, 1987, 21-35.
This reports on a series of tank tests carried out at the Southampton Institute on six representative 'A' Class models, one from each decade of the class's existence, starting with Daniels' *Crusader* of 1924 and ending with Stollery's *Lollipop* of 1977.

Despite the wide variation in hull shape and other characteristics of the models tested, the conclusion is that the measured differences between the different designs in the tank are very small. The small differences between these test results and the much wider variation in observed sailing performance are attributed to factors not measured by the tank tests, particularly changes in the efficiency of sail plans, which reflected improvements in the available materials and better understanding of the underlying aerodynamics.

29   COLEMAN, H S: *Model Making for Boys*: London,
English Universities Press, (Junior Teach
Yourself Series), 1949: 88, 4º.

Coleman was editor of the *Modelcraft Magazine* and appears
also to have been the owner of the Modelcraft business empire.
There is an enthusiastic introduction that suggests that model
making is the most wonderful occupation on earth and that the
simple projects that he offers in this book will inevitably lead on to
a lifetime of quiet satisfaction.

All the projects save one are drawn from the Modelcraft plans
catalogue and include a static galleon model, a waterline ship
model, a simple single cylinder steam plant, and 28 inch span
flying model and a solid $1/72$ model of an airliner.

The only project that is not from the catalogue is the 'toy
yacht'. This is a 16 inches model of quite exemplary crudity. The
hull is solid, the rig (in 1949), is a simple gaff sloop. The whole
thing is pretty pathetic and there is no rudder..

30   COLLETT, David: *Recollections of Model Yacht
Sailing at Southwold*: Southwold, Collett, 1989, 35,
25cm.

An informal history of the Southwold Model Yacht Regattas, which
have been conducted in the town during the summer holiday period
since the 1890s. Originally there were two competing series, one
run by the town council and the other by the company that ran the
pier. The organisation has since the 1920s been in the hands of a
group of families that holiday in the town on a regular basis.

This is a niche activity in model sailing which produces a
steady flow of new designs to meet its own rather special demands,
some by participants, others by designers active in mainstream
model yachting. It has also preserved in use some boats that date
back to the 1920s and earlier. Even more important than its
preservation of old boats, it has preserved a style of competition
and organisation that have been totally superseded in the
mainstream sport. David Collett, who died in 1998, had himself
been a regular participant since his childhood.

The most important material is in the photo illustrations,
some from the very early years, but most depicting recent activity.

31   CREATOR, (pseud*): Model Ships and Boats (Model Engineering Series, No 3)*: London, Bear, Wilson, 1944: 32, oblong 8º.

Though the author's pseudonym appears in the bibliographical references, it is nowhere to be found on the book. That an author should write under a pseudonym and then take even his pseudonym off the book suggests a deep uncertainty about the value of what he has written. An entirely justified doubt.

There are three projects, of which only the first is for a sailing model, a 63 cm. long, box-like, flat bottom sharpie made from plywood.

This is a shoddy piece of book making, cheaply produced, with drawings that are tiny, messy and confusing. The first page contains a number of important misprints that make nonsense of the advice on the sizes of plywood from which the boat is to be constructed. Dimensions are sometimes in metric, sometimes in imperial units. The design, methods of construction and general approach are crude and inadequate. Sailmaking is treated in half a line, ballasting with the sentence 'Fasten a piece of lead to the bottom of the boat so that it floats on its water line.'

This is one of a series of 'Model Engineering' titles from this publisher; those on aeromodelling and railway modelling are equally dire.

*32   CURTI, Orazio: *Modelli Navali; Enciclopedia delle Modellismo Navale (Biblioteca del Mare, No 8; Manuale Tecnica e Sport, No. 4)*: Milan, A Mursia, 1968: 599, 4°.
3rd edition, 1970: 545, 4°.
4th edition, 1971: 543, 4°.

As *Modèles Reduits*: Paris, Editions Maritime et d'Outre-Mer, 1971: 528, 4°.

As *Schiffsmodellbau*: Rostock, Hinsdorff, VEB, 1972: 520, 4°.

As *Schiffsmodellbau*: Bielefeld/Berlin, Delius Klasing, 1973: 520, 4°.
2nd edition, 1974: 3rd edition, 1975:
4th edition, 1977: 5th edition,1979:
6th edition, 1982: 7th edition, 1987
8th edition ('sonderausgabe'), 1992

As *Varende Scheepsmodellen*: Bussum, De Boer Maritiem, 1986: 8°, 25 cm.

This is an encyclopaedic coverage of all forms of marine modelling. At the time of its first appearance Curti was Vice President of the Italian Marine Modellers Association and director of the transport collections in the Museum of Technology in Milan. The main thrust is towards glass case scale models.

The space devoted to model yachts is limited, only 30-odd pages; a large part of the material is taken without acknowledgement from British sources, but the book is important as the 'Trojan Horse'[7] by which British practice, particularly the use of the vane gear, was given really wide diffusion in Europe. There are no drawings big enough to build from, but many of the illustrative lines plans are lifted from **Priest and Lewis** (No. 115).

The German editions, though published separately in the DDR and BRD, were all apparently printed in the East. The Dutch edition divides the original up into three separate titles, of which the one noted extracts the material on practical models, both sail and power.

---

[7] We owe this telling phrase to Gerd Menkens.

*33   DANIELS , William John & Herbert Boswell
TUCKER: *Model Sailing Craft*: London, Chapman
& Hall, New York, Rudder Publishing Co., 1932:
xii, 246, 4°.
2nd, Revised 'cheaper' edition: London,
Chapman & Hall, New York, Rudder
Publishing, 1939: xii, 196, 4°.

3rd, 'New' edition: London, Chapman & Hall,
Cambridge MA, Cornell Maritime, 1952: xii,
240, 4°.

This is the classic work, embodying the design, construction and
sailing practice of Bill Daniels, the premier model yachtsman of his
generation, and a man with a good claim to be the inventor of
model yachting in its modern form. Though a joint work,
comparison with the solo writing of the two authors suggests that
Daniels did the work and Tucker looked over his shoulder and
wrote down what he did. Tucker was however so much in thrall to
Daniels' concepts that it is often hard to tell their later work apart.

There is comprehensive coverage of all aspects of design and
construction, both by Daniels' preferred bread and butter system
and plank-on-frame. Here also is the only written description of
sail making in cotton that comes anywhere close to enabling a
beginner to do it. There is a careful treatment of fittings and their
manufacture and a detailed coverage of sailing techniques. As well
as encapsulating the high technology of model yachting in the
1930s, it remains by far the best 'how to do it' book for the wooden
boat with cotton sails.

The first edition contains some material on sailing models
other than class racing yachts, but this disappears from the later
editions, as does the wealth of photographs of early 'A' boats that
adorn the first. The 1939 edition is relatively rare, as most of the
copies were destroyed by fire in the warehouse during the war. The
1952 edition contains some treatment of the use of the vane in
competition, together with a design for a vane gear, but this is not
as helpful as articles that Daniels was writing in the periodicals at
the same period. There is also a discussion of the place of radio in
model yachting that can, with hindsight, be seen to have been well
off the point. D&T did not progress beyond envisaging it as a way
of dispensing with the mate in the pond sailing competition with
which they were familiar.

Each edition contains a fresh set of designs to the current
Model Yachting Association classes; in the first these include

Crusader, the 'A' boat with which Daniels won the *Yachting Monthly* Cup for Scott Freeman in 1924 and 25, as well as one non-class design. The other designs in each edition were prepared specially for the book.

*34   **DANIELS, William John & Herbert Boswell TUCKER:** *Build Your Boy a Model Yacht: with Full Size Construction Plans*: **London, Marine Models, 1936: 68, 8°.**

*35   **DANIELS, William John & Herbert Boswell TUCKER:** *Build Your Boy a Model Yacht*: **London, Marine Models, 1938: 84, 8°.**

*36   **DANIELS, William John & Herbert Boswell TUCKER:** *Build Yourself a Model Yacht*: **London, Percival Marshall, 1950: xi, 84, 8°.**

These are essentially the same book in three different guises. They give a thorough coverage of construction techniques, but with no design discussion. The first version is arranged around the building of a 30 inch sloop by bread and butter methods. Possibly this size was chosen to fit the 30 inch class that the MYA had tried to get off the ground in the early thirties, though it was effectively dead in the water by the time of the first publication.

Though linked to a small boat, the methods described are entirely typical of Daniels' practice for larger models. Lines of the boat are given as well as full size cutting diagrams for the lifts. Reports from those who have built this boat suggest that, quite exceptionally for Daniels, it is less than perfectly balanced. There is also a brief treatment of sailing techniques and of the organisation of the sport.

The 1938 version and the post war edition, which are aimed more at adults building for themselves, substitute a 36 inch Restricted class design for the 30 inch boat and add a 30 inch sharpie to be built in plywood. The lines and cutting diagrams are retained. The first two versions are card backed, but the final edition is a hard back.

*37   **DANIELS, William John & Herbert Boswell TUCKER:** *Model Sailing Yachts*: **London, Percival Marshall, 1951: 132, 8°.**

This was designed by Marshall as a replacement for his long lasting, but by 1951 seriously outdated, **Model Sailing Yachts** (No. 94), that for most of its life had been a Daniels text. This is very similar in approach to the earlier **Model Sailing Craft** (No. 33), but without any design discussion or treatment of the design process. The plans are limited to the three 'simpler' and more popular Model Yachting Association classes (10-rater, 'M' and 36R). They were available as full size prints from the Marshall plans service.

The construction material is sound and comprehensive, but the discussion of sailing technique is extremely abbreviated. The coverage of the principles and use of vane gear for instance is barely a single page.

*38   **DARLING, Thomas: *Miniature Racing Yachts and How to Build Them*: New York and London, Charles Scribner's Sons, 1936: 118, oblong folio.**

A large landscape format book. A US treatment of the usual run of construction and rigging, but unusually well set out. Darling was a marine engineer and boat builder, who became a crafts teacher in schools. He wrote on construction in magazines of the 1930s and this is the collected and collated works.

There is discussion of some US designs of steering gear, competitors to the Braine gear. The lines plans balance between boats to the home grown Model Yacht Racing Association of America (MYRAA) classes of the 1920s and the International classes which at that period only a minority of US skippers sailed. They include some smallish boats to US Rules ('R' and 'D' classes), by Darling. These date from the 1920s. There is also an uncredited 'A' boat, presumably by Darling, and a design for a 6-metre that, from its style and layout, looks as though it might have been contributed by a Brit. If so, it is very probably by H B Tucker. Surprisingly, given its date, the book contains no mention of the burgeoning Marblehead Class.

The book contains measurement details of a number of early competitors in the Gosport international races.

39   **DAVIS, Charles, (Consulting Editor): *Harper's Boating Book for Boys*: New York and London, Harper Brothers, (Harper's Young People Library), 1912.**

We have not seen this. It is said to be a guide to full size motor boating, rowing, canoeing and sailing craft, which also includes a couple of chapters on model sailing craft. There is no copy in the British Library.

40   DAVIES, John and Chris JACKSON: *An*
             Introduction to Marine Modelling: Upton-on-
             Severn, Traplet, 1995: ISBN: 0 9510589 5 9: 82,
             25cm.

A very basic introduction to all forms of marine modelling. There is only one chapter on sailing models, with no discussion of either design or construction. The chapter on competition is little more than directions on how to contact the various national authorities.

41   DEASON, Geoffrey Heath and Douglas Arthur
             RUSSELL: *The Model Boat Book*: Leighton
             Buzzard, Drysdale Press, 1950, 8°.

This is essentially a collection of plans and 'how to do it' information from a leading publisher of model magazines of the period. It's not clear whether all the material appeared in magazine form initially, but some of it certainly did. It covers both sail and power, with only four sail designs. Only one of these is for a class boat, an 'M', *Merlin*, by L A Garrett, a Birmingham skipper.

This is a conventional design reflecting the ideas that were current in the immediate post war period. The other sail designs are for two centreboard dinghies, and a semi-scale hard chine cruiser, also with a CB. These are all three by the team of M Cowell and A Palmer, of whom we know nothing except that they clearly had a love affair with the drop keel.

42   DOUGLAS, George Bruce et al: *The Ship Model*
             Book. How to Build and Rig Model Ships, with a
             Special set of Paper Patterns for the famous ship
             Benjamin F Packard: New York, Rudder Publishing
             Co., 1926: 32, 30cm.
             2nd edition, ...*with a chapter on American*
             Clipper Ships and the lines and plans of a New
             Bedford Whaler: 1926: 47, 30cm.

             3rd edition, 1926: 47, 30cm.

We have not seen a copy of any of the three quite distinct editions of this work which, curiously, all appeared in a single year. It may well prove to be given over entirely to glass case scale models.

*43   **DRURY, Jack, with Interpolations and Commentary by Russell POTTS and Richard HOWLETT: *Jack's Guide to the Restoration of Older Model Yachts*: London, The Curved Air Press, 1999: ISBN: 1 873148 09 7: 38, 21cm.**

Jack Drury was a member of the Bournville club in Birmingham from 1926 until his death in 1990. He was also a member of the Vintage Group. Shortly before his death, he wrote some rather disorganised and incomplete notes on restoration for the benefit of his fellow members. They are based substantially on his own restoration in 1949 of his 10-rater *Opal*, first built in 1934.

This work is his notes, expanded to include contributions from two other VG members with extensive experience of restoration projects.

44   *ENCYCLOPAEDIA BRITANNICA*:

11th edition, Edinburgh, 1910.

13th edition, Chicago, IL, 1929.

As always, the 11th edition proves superior to all other versions. It carries (for the first time) a brief article on 'Model Yachting' in addition to a more conventional entry on 'Models', which treats of the use of models as design aids in various types of engineering. The model yachting piece is well informed and competent within its limits of space. It points the reader seeking further information to the two most recent serious books on the subject. It is unsigned and may have been written by someone more familiar with full size competitive practice than model racing, since he assumes that modellers conducted their races on a handicap basis.

The later edition has no separate model yachting entry and the short 'Models' article, written by W J Bassett-Lowke, attempts to cover all uses of models, together with the commercial production of models as toys; it is so concerned to give a space to extolling an unnamed 'large producer of all forms of models based in Northampton' that it contains no mention of competitive model based sports. More modern editions contain no useful material.

A brief trawl through the encyclopaedias on the open shelves of the British Library shows that no other in a European language contains anything of interest, with the exception of the *Larousse du XXme Siècle* (Paris, 1928). In this, while the article on *'modèle'* hardly mentions models of the sort we are interested in, there is a delightful vignette of a skipper in a straw hat about to launch an absolutely huge model yacht on to what is clearly the *Eau Suisse* at Versailles. This must date from well before the date of publication.

*45   FARLEY, Charles H, edited by William Earl
BOEBERT, Afterword by Rod CARR: *Building
Planked Models. A Manual of Vintage Model Yacht
Construction*: Albuquerque NM, US Vintage Model
Yacht Group, 1997: 114, 4º.
London, The Curved Air Press, 1998: 114,
25cm.

This is a nicely produced reprint of articles that appeared
originally in 1940 in *The Model Craftsman*, and again in 1945 in
Model Yachting Monthly, the journal of the MYRAA (No. 233),
which Farley edited.

The material has been reorganised to give a more coherent
presentation than was possible in its original form as disparate
articles, but apart from this and a few footnotes, what you get is
what Farley wrote. The techniques described represent the normal
technology of the period. The methods are clearly described and, so
far as any written text can tell you how to do it, they will permit a
reasonably assiduous beginner to complete a boat.

Rod Carr's afterword touches briefly on how to update these
techniques for modern materials and modern adhesives.

*46   FISHER, Herbert et al: *How to Build a Model
Yacht*: New York, Rudder Publishing, 1902: 44, 4º.
Reprinted, 1917: 44, 4º.

This is a collection of articles and designs that originally appeared
in *The Rudder*, a magazine devoted to the full size sport, during
the 1890s. As well as the usual construction material, there is
coverage of the automatic steering gears then in use in the New
York area, which, though relatively sophisticated in their
arrangements, are still basically reverse tiller gears. There are
several designs to American Rules of the day, including what is
probably the first published design by the long lived and prolific
Walter R Many, as well as some British 10-rater designs of the
period. We have not seen the 1902 edition, but we have no reason
to suppose that it differs from the 1917 reprint.

It is interesting as evidence of the extent to which model
yachtsmen at this period made use of full size yachting magazines,
on both sides of the Atlantic, to disseminate their ideas and
designs.

47   GILMORE, Horace Herman: *The Junior Boat Builder*: New York, MacMillan, 1938: Reprinted, 1951.

We have not been able to find a copy of this. We suspect that it may be very similar to the following item.

48   GILMORE, Horace Herman: *Model Boats for Beginners*: New York, Harper Bros, 1959: viii, 98, 8º.

This wide ranging volume is aimed at absolute beginners and juvenile beginners at that. It is extremely simplistic in its view of model making, as in its parochial view of the world. The list of notable dates in shipping history includes almost no event occurring outside the USA and the Blue Riband gets its first mention in 1952, when it is held for the first time by a US registered vessel. The models of powered craft are crude and have no power plants; they seem best adapted to bath time play. The sail models are equally crude, but do have sails and might be persuaded to sail, though there is no discussion of how this might be achieved.

49   GOEPFERICH, W: *Wir bauen Schiffsmodelle: Die Modellsegelyacht 'Wiking'*: Stuttgart, Franckh, 1941.

We have not seen this title. It is, with the work of **de Bruycker**, **Zwalgun** and others, part of an efflorescence of model yacht publishing in Germany during the war years. Most of this took the form of the publication of individual full size plans with little or no accompanying text. We have only been able to see the plans of **Tiller**, published by Maier, and cannot determine from the bibliographical sources alone exactly what the other designs were. Some however were clearly for competitive models. At least six designers and five different publishers were active in this market between 1941 and 1943.

50   GRAHAM, P Anderson: *Country Pastimes for Boys*: London, Longman's, 1893: xvi, 448, 8º.

A huge compendium of things for a schoolboy to do when at home in the country, 'thrown upon his own resources, away from school and lively companions'. More than half the text is concerned with specifically country pursuits; pets, angling, poultry raising and the like. It includes over 100 pages on bird's nesting alone; by comparison 'Toy Boat Making and Sailing' gets only 10 pages, but it includes the information that

...in the past many schools used to race model boats on one afternoon a week and the boys would build their own boats. Now the manufacture of toy boats has become such an industry that it is easier to go to a toy shop and few will take the trouble to carve a boat for them selves.

The boat proposed is small, only twelve inches long, and is to be carved by eye from a single block of white pine. The style is more of an open boat than a yacht, with thwarts and no decking. The rig is a low gaff sloop. Only at the stage of setting up the rig, is it suggested that a strip of lead or zinc tacked to the bottom of the boat may be necessary.

Despite the rather cavalier approach to some of the basics, the article assumes that the reader will want to build other and better boats and includes some engravings showing full size Solent small raters as an inspiration for the design experiments he expects his reader to undertake.

*51   **GREEN, George Colman:** *The Model Yacht Club*
         Guide and Directory: **Norwich, Green, 1908: 96, 8⁰.**
This little book, assembled and collated by a very young and somewhat eccentric enthusiast who was the founding secretary of the Norfolk and Norwich MYC, is based upon a mail survey of the clubs that then existed, supplemented by a deal of hopeful and outdated information about the clubs that did not reply to his enquiries, together with arguments for the establishment of a national authority for model yachting. In among the duff information, the endearing misprints and the energetic riding of editorial hobby horses, there is a wealth of information about the size, activity and interests of the fifty or so clubs that made substantial replies.

It was published by the author with the support of a committee of guarantors and was originally offered at a shilling. It failed to sell very widely and the price was quickly reduced to sixpence, probably at the insistence of the guarantors. It is extremely rare. There are no copies in the copyright libraries and we know of only two extant examples.

*52   GRIFFIN, Roy: *Model Racing Yacht Construction*:
Hemel Hempstead, MAP, 1973: ISBN: 0 85242 347 0:
112, 21cm.
2nd, revised edition, Hemel Hempstead, Argus,
1979: 120, 21cm.

This was originally a long series of articles that appeared in *Model
Boats* in 1970-71. It gives full coverage to the range of construction
techniques of the day, with the exception of bread and butter, but
including glass reinforced plastic moulding. Great pains are taken
to ensure that the instructions leave nothing to chance and that
everything can only be done the right way. There is equally careful
treatment of spars and fittings and of final assembly.

In its day, this was the last word on how to build and prepare
a model for serious competition. Now it is a useful record of the
state of construction technology at the end of the free sailing era,
before the impact of radio control began to change the design and
construction parameters. The second edition includes a brief
treatment of radio installation, but has not fully taken on board the
implications of the radio revolution. The clear and concise chapter
on sail making is by George CLARK, and covers the construction of
single panel sails in hot rolled terylene.

53   GRIMWOOD, V R: *American Ship Models and How
to Build Them*: New York, Norton, 1943: 188, 4º.
Reprinted, New York, Bonanza Books, n. d.
(1960s?): 188, 4º.

This is primarily a collection of plans for scale, glass case, models of
historically significant vessels, with fairly brief instructions on how
they might be built. One project however is for a Marblehead.
Examination of the plan reveals it to be an unacknowledged steal
from the 'M' design offered in the 1939 edition of Daniels and
Tucker's *Model Sailing Craft* (No. 33). The discussion of the plan
and the background of model yachting makes clear that Grimwood
was not a model yachtsman.

54   GROSVENOR, J du V: *Model Yachts and Boats:*
Designing, Making and Sailing: London, J Upcott
Gill (Bazaar & Mart), 1882: vi, 183, 8⁰.
US edition, New York, Rudder Publishing Co,
1891. reprinted, Rudder, 1898.

2nd English edition, London, Upcott Gill, 1905,
xii, 204, 8⁰.

'Cheap edition', London, Bazaar, Exchange
and Mart, 1910: 183, 8⁰.

> Van Stockum records another US edition as
> 'New York, Scribner's, n. d.'. We have not seen
> it and it does not appear in the *National Union
> Catalog*, nor in the New York Public Library
> *Guide*. The 1891 *Rudder* edition appears to be
> the real thing.

Though this followed closely upon Biddle's pioneering work of 1879,
and Biddle claimed he had been plagiarised by an unnamed author,
the book is substantially different in several respects from his. In
general Grosvenor is not very interested in racing models. At one
point he remarks that for a racing craft rather different proportions
would be needed, but he does not elaborate on this, let alone give a
lines plan of such a boat.

Such design drawings as there are, are small and some are
deficient. In one case there are more sections in the body plan than
section lines in the sheer plan. They might be just about adequate
to build from. With one exception, they give the lines of full size
types of craft suggested as suitable for models. The building
techniques he suggests are different in several respects from those
of Biddle and seem over engineered and likely to produce an
unnecessarily heavy model.

Unlike Biddle, however, he gives over a third of his space to
the discussion of design considerations and the theory underlying
choices of proportions and the like.

The publisher's advertisements in the rear of the first edition
suggest that at this period *Bazaar, Exchange and Mart*, which then
appeared three times a week, carried editorial matter on 'practical
subjects', as well as its mainstay of small classified advertisements.
If so, it is possible that some of Grosvenor's material had appeared
there earlier. We have not yet had an opportunity to verify this.

*55   GROSVENOR, J du V, (revised by Edward Walter
       HOBBS): *Model Yachts and Boats: Designing,*
       Building and Sailing: London, Bazaar, Exchange
       & Mart, 1923: xii, 204, 8º.

This is something of a curiosity, written when Hobbs was
freelancing as a technical author and taking any contract he could
get. He wrote on home decorating and many other topics besides
modelling, as well as running a plans service and designing
powered models for Bassett-Lowke.

The book spatchcocks together material from the original
Grosvenor text with material that is very similar to what was in
Hobbs' own *Model Sailing Boats* (No. 68) that appeared the same
year. Some of the original Grosvenor plans survive alongside
Hobbs' own plans for a 10-rater, a 12-metre and a 24 inch non-class
model. There is also some material on power boats and on glass
case models. The photo illustrations give excellent atmospheric
shots of the London model yachting scene just before 1914.

56   HAINERT, L E: *How to Make a Cat Boat*:
       Elizabeth, NJ, Practical Arts, 1927?

57   HAINERT, L E: *How to Make a 25 inch Model*
       Yacht: Elizabeth, NJ, Practical Arts, 1928?

These two titles appear in the *Cumulative Book Index*, and the
National Union Catalog, but we have not succeeded in locating
them. They appear to be part of the material associated with
schools Industrial Arts programs.

58   HALL, Cyril: *Models and How to Make Them*:
       London, Pearson, 1906: xiv, 138, 8º.

59   HALL, Cyril: *Model Making*: London, Pearson,
       1909: xiv, 138, 8º.

       **This is recorded by the British Library catalogue
       as a '2nd edition', but is, apart from the title page,
       identical to the previous title.**
       New York, Fenner & Co., 1910:

       3rd edition, London, Pearson, 1919: xiv, 138, 8º.

Despite the changes of title and the separate editions, all the UK
titles are identical, and we assume the US edition is also.

This is a deeply disappointing book. The cover illustrations
include a small but practical sailing model, in the style of the
'superior toy boats' featured in catalogues published by Stephens's
and other model engineers of the period. The text is mainly
concerned with the usual run of steam engines, electric motors and

the like. The final chapter, of four pages only, deals with sailing models and the treatment is derisory. There are no drawings in the yacht chapter, except a general arrangement to show the intended sail plan. We assume the chapter is there because a general title on models was not thought to be complete without a sailing boat.

60   HARLEY, Basil: 'The Society of Arts Model Ship Trials, 1758-63' in *Transactions of the Newcomen Society*, 63, (1991-2), 53-72.

A brief account of an attempt to improve the design of RN men of war and frigates by means of a Society of Arts competition for new hull designs in the form of models. These were put through comparative trials, being towed both in smooth water and on a pond in Epping Forest which was intended to provide a rough water trial. In this latter trial the models were fitted with sails to provide a steadying effect and thus a more realistic assessment of their behaviour in a seaway.

61   HARLEY, Basil: *Toy Boats (Shire Album No.193)*: Aylesbury, Shire Publications, 1987: 32, 21 cm.

A brief survey of toy boats, almost exclusively concerned with commercially produced, tinplate, semi-scale models powered by clockwork or simple steam plants. There is passing mention of commercial sailing models, but nothing of substance.

62   HARMON, F Ward: *Ship Models Illustrated*: New York, Marine Model Co., 1943.

We have not seen this.

63   HASLUCK, Paul Nooncree (ed*): Cassell's
            Cyclopaedia of Mechanics, containing Receipts
            Processes and Memoranda for Workshop use.
            Based on Personal Experience and Expert
            Knowledge*: London, Cassell, originally as a
            weekly part work, collected in four volumes, each
            of approx 380 pages, titled, 'First series', etc., 1900-
            1905, 4º.
            Revised and expanded edition, with the index
            in a separate volume; five volumes, each
            approx 350 pages, Cassell, 1908, 4º.

            There is also an undated 'Special
            edition'under the London imprint of The
            Waverley Book Co.

This was published as a multi-volume compendium in 1900-1905,
but was originally a part work. The introduction emphasises that
all the material has been supplied in answer to queries and
expanded in the light of responses from 'practical men' to the
original reply. Almost certainly this is a compilation from the
weekly replies to readers carried in **Work** (No. 249) and other
similar journals published by Cassell.

There are claimed to be 27,000 'items', all carefully indexed.
Of these, a mere seven relate to sailing models. Most of these offer
sail plans for enquirers' existing hulls. The paragraphs are
extremely brief, and despite a reference to 'the new Rule' (which
turns out to be the Linear Rating Rule of 1896), there is little
evidence that the respondents are offering 'expert knowledge' on
the best model yachting practice of the day.

The Waverley edition, of which we have seen only a few pages
in photocopy, may have been an early example of a promotional
offer to stimulate newspaper or magazine circulation,

64   HASLUCK, Paul Nooncree (ed): *Building Model
            Boats, including Sailing and Steam Vessels*:
            London, Cassell, (*Work* Handbooks) 1899: 160, 8º.
            Reprinted 1901, 1914.

            Philadelphia, David McKay, 1906.

Work was a general craft magazine, published by Cassell from the
mid 1880s, which occasionally contained model yachting material.
Unlike Percival Marshall's **Model Engineer** it was, until well into
the twentieth century, aimed at a professional, rather than a
gentleman amateur readership. There was a long series of

handbooks, most of which were clearly intended to improve the practice of their artisan readers, but there were occasional titles that dealt with the technical diversions of the better class of working man, of which this is an example.

The 1899 edition is clearly the work of several hands, and is probably drawn from material that appeared earlier in *Work* and other Cassell journals. The plans for a cutter and a schooner appeared in the first volume of *Amateur Mechanics*. The contents also include a steam powered model of a transatlantic liner of the 1880s and some treatment of glass case models. This last includes a revolving disc device to allow the 'sea' in a glass case to give the impression of movement.

There is a later version of this handbook, edited by **Bernard JONES** and largely written by **Edward W HOBBS** (No. 82)

65   **HEIGHWAY, G:** *A Fast Sailing Yacht*: **London, Modelcraft, 1944.**

This appears in the *Cumulative Book Index*, but, as with a number of other Modelcraft titles of the period, seems not to have reached the British Library. We have not seen a copy, but, on the evidence of other titles published by Modelcraft during the war, we assume that it was a brief 'how to do it' text describing a relatively small model sailing yacht.

66   **HOBBS, Edward Walter:** 'Boat, How to make a Model', in *Cassell's Household Encyclopaedia*, Vol. I, 405-6: London, Cassell, n. d., but early 1920s.

An extremely short article that covers both a small sailing boat and a steam powered scale model. The colour plate of drawings is quite good and would enable an experienced craftsman to build a boat. The sailing yacht design is a typical gaff rigged sloop and very similar to the standard commercial product from any time in the preceding thirty years. The written instructions are so abbreviated that in the hands of a beginner they could never result in a completed boat. The encyclopaedia contains a similar article by Hobbs on model aircraft.

*67   HOBBS, Edward Walter (ed): *Wonderful Models*:
London, Percival Marshall, 1928: two vols, 1152,
8⁰.
Originally a part work issued in 18 monthly
parts, 1927-28, but arranged as an
encyclopaedia, and intended to be collected
into two alphabetical volumes. Published in
this form, 1928.

A large compendium on all aspects of model making. Distributed
through the work are a number of articles on model yachting,
including pieces by the Marquis of Ailsa, who was then the patron
of the Model Yachting Association, and by H B Tucker, the then
Chairman. There are brief articles on the Rating Rules, on
construction methods, sail making and on the theoretical bases of
design, but most are too slight to be of real value. Some pieces are
signed by contributors, others are anonymous, and presumably by
Hobbs himself.

There are a small number of designs, including the very
successful 18 footer *Thistle* of 1923, an 'A' boat *June* and a 10-rater
Vicuña. All are by A W Littlejohn and the last two are said to be
'prepared especially for *Wonderful Models*'. They were available
as full size plans from Marshall's plans service and do not appear
to have been published elsewhere.

*68   HOBBS, Edward Walter: *Model Sailing Boats:
Their Design, Building and Sailing*: London,
Cassell, New York, Funk and Wagnall, 1923: 312,
8⁰.
2nd 'Revised' edition, 1929: 312, 8⁰.

Reprinted, 1935, 1939, 1941 (the 1941 printing
is described as a '5th edition', but it does not
differ from the 2nd of 1929).

Reprint of 1929 edition, New York, Funk and
Wagnall, ('Newton K Gregg, Publisher', The
Gregg Series of Reprints on Crafts and
Hobbies), 1971: 312, 8⁰.

Hobbs was a multi-talented man, naval architect, engineer and an
endlessly innovative entrepreneur. He was employed as the
manager of Bassett-Lowke's shop in Holborn when it opened in
1908. While in this position he became the founding Secretary of
the Model Yacht Racing Association (MYRA) in 1911. The
foundation meeting was held in a tea shop two doors along from

Bassett's. Before 1914 he had published what was for its generation the standard work on model power boats and this is his parallel work on sailing models. The material nearly all relates to pre-war practice and publication must have been delayed by the war.

It gives extended coverage of design considerations and design procedures, as well as good detail on construction and rigging. This includes a number of uncommon methods, including construction in metal, in canvas and in paper, as well as moulding in rubber and concrete. This last anticipates in model scale the ferro-concrete techniques used by some full size builders after 1945.

The photo illustrations, not as well reproduced as those in Hobbs' revision of **Grosvenor**, (No. 55), almost all relate to the pre-war period. They include an illustration of 'an Argentine 12-metre', but it is not clear whether it was designed there or built in England for an Argentine client; either way, interesting evidence of serious model sailing in South America, long before the advent of radio controlled competition.

The lines drawings are more up to date, but small and difficult to work from; they include, in the second edition, a total of 14, covering a very wide range of class and non-class boats. The diagrams of fittings and rigging arrangements are particularly clear and give good guidance on the practice of serious competitive modellers around the time of the 1914-18 war.

69   HOBBS, Edward Walter: *Model Racing Yachts*: (Cassell's Model Maker Series): London, Cassell, 1934: 62, 8º.

70   HOBBS, Edward Walter (revised by N G TAYLOR): *Model Racing Yachts*: London, (Cassell's New Modelmaker Series no. 4) 1954: 72, 8º.

Both versions of this title, one of Cassell's popular model making series, are relatively slight works, aimed at schoolboys and beginners, rather than the committed model yachtsman. There is no design discussion, but brief treatment of the main methods of construction. The 1934 version covers carving, bread and butter and plank-on-frame, as well as very cursory treatment of sail making and fittings. The designs (by Hobbs) are all for non-class boats and most are in small, beginners' sizes. Full size drawings were available from the publisher.

The revision by Taylor carries forward some of the plans from the 1934 edition, and adds, rather unexpectedly, the plans of an 'A' boat, *Pandora,* a 10-rater, *Allegro,* and an unnamed Marblehead.

All are by Harry Andrews, at that time a member of the Newcastle club and later MYA Secretary. *Pandora* was a successful boat in her day and has recently come to light again in remarkably good condition. *Allegro* was also a successful boat and an example of the design was still sailing at Newcastle in the early 1990s.

71   HORST, Claude William: *Model Sail and Power Boats*: **Milwaukee, WI, Bruce Publishing, 1933: 96, 8°.**
         2nd 'Revised and Enlarged' edition,
         Milwaukee, WI, Bruce Publishing 1939: 104, 8°.

We have not seen this. Horst was a crafts teacher in Milwaukee schools and wrote a number of titles on boat models for use in school shop programs. This is the earliest and contains, among other things, plans and construction details for a 25 inch sloop model, which were reproduced in the USVMYG journal *The Model Yacht*, (No. 266) Vol 2. No. 1, (Spring 1998), pp17-22.

72   HORST, Claude William: *Model Boats for Boys*: **Peoria, IL, Manual Arts Press, 1935: 47, 4°.**
We have not seen this. Another treatment of model boats in the high school shop program.

73   HORST, Claude William: *Model Boats for Juniors*: **Chicago, IL and Milwaukee, WI, Bruce Publishing, 1936: 78, 4°.**
         Reprinted, 1939.

This is the only one of Horst's junior titles we have been able to examine, though we suspect that there is a deal of commonality between them. More chips from the shop program, with a number of simple projects for juniors. Most are for small semi-scale power models. The sailboat projects are mostly small and very simple, but would probably be quite effective on the water. The 25 inch sloop from his first book reappears here. There is a brief treatment of sailing techniques, which makes it clear that Horst intended his boats to be sailed properly.

*74   HORST, Claude William: *A Marblehead Model Sailing Yacht*: **Milwaukee, WI, Bruce Publishing, 1939: 40, 4°.**
This is the last in time of Horst's books for crafts teachers, and the only one that deals with a serious class racing yacht project. It gives comprehensive coverage of the building of a Marblehead by his signature method, bread and butter, but with all the lifts also joined on the centre line. The design itself is very typical of US practice of the period. There is sensible coverage of fittings

manufacture and rig details, as well as sailing technique, but nothing on sail making.

*75 **HOULE, Thomas J:** *Building and Racing Radio Control Sailboats*: **Waukesha, WI, Kalmbach, 1993: 63, 4°.**

This is an American treatment of modern radio controlled sailing boats. It covers building from kits, and a wide selection of scratch building techniques, including traditional bread and butter, glass reinforced plastic sheathing over balsa, glass reinforced plastic moulding, cold moulded veneer, *papier maché* and vacuum moulding. There is detailed treatment of radio installation in the US style with lever arm winches and a radio board mounted in the bottom of the hull, as well as rigging detail. There is brief guidance on sail making in modern materials, but the reader is referred to more detailed material in the **AMYA** *Quarterly*. There is also some treatment of the basics of radio racing.

There are no plans as such, and much of the text is devoted to non class sailing models of various types.

76 **HUMPHREY, Richard V:** *Building Fibreglass Ship Models*: **Blue Ridge Summit, PA, TAB, 1970.**

We have not seen this. Unlike a large number of TAB titles it was not published in the UK. It may not be concerned with sailing models.

77 **ICKIS, Marguerite:** *Handicrafts and Hobbies for Pleasure and Profit*: **New York, Greystone Press, 1948:**

A 'how to' book covering a wide range of crafts, including fly tying and model making, with brief chapters on the modelling of cars, trains, boats and planes. Not a very serious contribution to the literature.

78 **JACKSON, Albert and David DAY:** *The Modelmaker's Handbook; An Illustrated Manual of 1,000 Techniques for Making All Types of Models Miniatures and Dioramas*: **London, Pelham, 1981, 1987; 352, 8°.**
New York, Knopf, 1981: 352, 8°.

A massively wide ranging coverage of every type of modelling activity: though originating in the UK it has a transatlantic feel and may have been intended from the outset as an international publishing venture. Boats come late on and there are only 24 pages to cover sail and power as well as some material on radio control. There is very brief coverage of the usual range of construction techniques as well as basic sailing concepts. Though brief, the information is generally sound, except that the authors have the curious idea that a carved hull is best hollowed out before the outside is shaped.

*79   **JACKSON, Chris:** *Radio Controlled Racing Yachts*: **Upton on Severn, Traplet Publications, 1997:   ISBN: 1 900371 15 4: 83, 25cm.**

Chris is currently editor of the general boat modelling magazine, *Marine Modelling International*, and has been an active model yachtsman since the 1960s.

This book aims to provide an introduction to modern competitive sailing and gives brief but authoritative treatment of the classes currently sailed, methods of construction for hull, rig and sails, together with equally brief treatment of radio installation, sail trim and race tactics in the light of the latest edition of the Racing Rules.

There are lots of line and photo illustrations, which give a good indication of the present state of the sport. Appendices give a world wide coverage of specialist suppliers and contact addresses for the national authorities affiliated to the Radio Sailing Division of the International Sailing Federation.

*80   **JEFFRIES, Cyril Robert:** *Radio Control for Model Yachts*: **Watford, Argus, 1974: ISBN: 0 85242 391 8: 112, 4º.**
2nd. 'revised' edition: Hemel Hempstead, Argus, 1977: 112, 4º.

This was the first, and for a long time the only, British publication to deal specifically with radio controlled yachting. It is rather disappointing.

Bob Jefferies, who died in 1988, was a professional electronics engineer and had been involved in radio flying before 1939 and worked on radio controlled target aircraft during the war. He had been involved in radio sailing for almost as long as it had existed in Britain, certainly from the early 1950s. His book draws so heavily on his own experience that it is almost a 'my life and hard times'. It tends to encapsulate the practice of his earlier days and was already a bit behind the game by the time it appeared.

He claimed that this was because his publishers had held it up for a couple of years in the press, but even had it appeared earlier, it would still have been out of date. Bob also tended to portray himself as more central to the development of the sport and more innovative than he in fact was.

That said, it is a valuable record of the state of the game in the early 1970s as radio yachting began to be a serious part of the sport in Britain and equipment specifically for yacht control teetered on the edge of commercial production. There are nostalgic illustrations of long forgotten first generation commercial sail winches.

81   **JOHNSON, Gene:** *Ship Model Building*: **New York, Cornell Maritime, 1944: 242, 24cm.**

              2nd edition, Cambridge MA, Cornell Maritime, 1953: 273, 24cm.

              3rd edition, 1961, 301, 24cm.

We have not seen this. Given its size, it may well include material on practical sailing models.

82   **JONES, Bernard (ed):** *Building Model Yachts, Sailing and Power*: **London, Cassell, (***Amateur Mechanic and Work* **Handbooks) 1924: 156, 8⁰.**

              Reprinted 1929, 1930, 1936.

This is the 1924 version of the **Work** handbook edited by **HASLUCK** (No. 64). It has a much more consistent tone than its predecessor and was mainly written by **HOBBS**, possibly in the form of articles in the magazine in the immediately preceding years. It retains the cutter design from 1899, though mainly to illustrate the principles of a lines drawing. In a more modern vein, there is a 10-r by Hobbs. In this version, the steam boat has also been updated and is now a flash steam powered hydroplane. There is again material on glass case models, closely parallel to Hobbs' writing elsewhere on clipper ship modelling.

83   **KIHLSTROM, Donald F:** *Sunday Sailors, a Beginner's Guide to Pond Boats and Model Yachting until the 1950s*: **Paducah, KY, Turner Publishing, 1998: ISBN: 1 56311 467 4: 144, 4⁰.**

This is the first book length treatment of model yachts as collectables. It is written by an antique dealer who specialises in the field, rather than by a model yachtsman, and at various points this shows. Its primary purpose is to act as a guide to collectors and it contains much valuable information on (mainly US) producers of the commercial toys which make up the bulk of the market.

It also attempts a brief history of model yachting in the US, up to the near demise of MYRAA in the 1950s. This is based largely on interviews with a small number of old and bold East Coast skippers and a review of the quite extensive toy trade periodical literature.

It presents what we see as a rather odd perspective, as the author has persuaded himself, not only that the really important action was in the toy boat field, but that the distinction between recreational sailing and the racing of class boats by MYRAA members was essentially one of class. Thus he sees the failure to 'democratise' the sport in the post war years as the reason for the fading away of MYRAA.

That said, the book contains much valuable information and a wealth of illustrations, both of collectable boats, (with a price guide) and of material from the scrapbooks of those he interviewed and from old books and magazines.

84   KINGSTON, William Henry Giles: *The Boy's Own Book of Boats, Including Vessels of Every Rig and Size, etc. together with Complete Instructions How to Make Sailing Models*: London, Sampson Low, 1861: ix, 224, 8º.
New edition, 'Revised Throughout': 1868: xii, 336, 8º.

reprinted, 1871 etc. with further revisions.

Essentially what the title suggests, a general coverage of maritime subjects by one of the most popular and most prolific boys' authors of the 19th century. Kingston was an early advocate of emigration to the Antipodean colonies. His fiction for boys is resolutely navalist and imperialist, well before either of these themes became universally popular. One series follows three naval officers from *Three Midshipmen* to *Three Admirals*.

The present book offers oblique evidence of the place of maritime and navalist concerns in the popular mind and the importance that Kingston attached to model sailing as a means of indoctrinating the younger generation. It discusses how to make small sailing models. Because it proposes using a commercial model as a pattern from which to make one's own, it gives a good picture of what was available in the middle years of the century, specifically the products of the Fleet Street Model Dockyard (see No. 96).

The second and subsequent editions also contain descriptions of model yachts designed and made by two builders on the Isle of Wight and sold through superior toy bazaars in London. They are quite different from the ideas that Kingston himself offers in the first edition, which follow full size practice quite closely. They are one of the earliest records of a specifically model line of development, independent of full size practice. Unfortunately, there are no lines plans and only the most meagre of illustrations specifically relating to models.

Though other material, for instance on naval developments, is kept up to date in each successive edition, the modelling coverage does not change after 1868.

The publishing history recorded above conceals a plethora of variant editions, bindings and printings, including three different 'first editions'. The British Library holdings are sparse compared to the number of editions and variants.

85   LA BERGE, Armand J: *Boats, Aeroplanes and Kites*: Peoria, IL, Manual Arts Press, 1935: 132. 2nd expanded edition, Peoria IL, Charles A Bennet Co., 1951: 155.

We have not been able to locate a copy of this title, but we are assured that it does deal with models, mainly in the context of the school Manual Arts Program. Toy says that it contains plans, building and sailing instructions. **KIHLSTROM** (No. 83) reveals that La Berge was a Manual Arts teacher in Minneapolis and ran extensive building and competitive programmes for local children.

86   LEEMING, *Toy Boats to Make at Home*: New York, Appleton-Century, 1946.

We have not seen this title.

87   LEITCH, Albert C: *Miniature Boat Building: the Construction of Working Models of Racing, Sail and Power Boats*: New York, Norman W Henley Publishing, 1928: xii, 242, 4°.

Leitch was a naval architect and author of other books on building powered models and the power plants for them. The designs in this book are linked to the supply of kits, or at least collections of suitable wood and fittings, by Boucher, who were one of the leading commercial suppliers in the US at that time. The text encourages the use of Boucher products and gives details of a number of patented devices which the firm had developed to facilitate the building and sailing of models.

The main emphasis is on power models, including the building of a steam plant of considerable complexity, but there are also four sail projects offered, with brief but competent instructions for their building. The designs are for two small and simple boats, a 20 inch cat boat and a 28 inch model closely based on the full size Star keel boat, which is described as 'the latest product of the Boucher shops'.

A more serious design is a 30 inch sloop, which is claimed to be designed by a naval architect (presumably not Leitch himself) and to be the result of long trials to determine the hull shape that was fastest and best suited for all round sailing. The content of these trials is not described. This is a round bottom hull and is to be carved from a single block of pine. The fin is a flat plate of galvanised iron and the rudder is operated by a simple reverse tiller gear. Despite the trials and the participation of a naval architect, this is still only a superior toy boat.

The final and most ambitious design is for a 36 inch hull of full keel form, similar to full size cruising yachts of the period. This is to be built by bread and butter methods and carries 9½ pounds of lead on her keel. She can be rigged either as a sloop or schooner. Despite the relative sophistication of this design, there is no real point of contact with what competitive model yachtsmen were doing at the time.

88   LESSEPS, M de: *Pond Models. Some Simple Thoughts on the Subject of Building and Sailing Them*: **Darien CT, Two Bytes Publishing, 1998, 47, 23 cm.**

A brief, simple and direct treatment of the subject. Perhaps a little short on technical detail and aiming only to produce practical small sailboats, rather than competitive models. The text is reproduced from MS, with charming illustrations taken from watercolours. It's not going to advance the state of the art, but you can see why a reviewer in the USVMYG's *Model Yacht* described it as 'inspirational'.

*89   LEWIS, John Arthur: *A Manual of Yacht Designs*: **Birmingham, Lewis, 1990: ISBN: 0 9516394 0 4: 192, oblong folio.**

This is a selection of John's designs since he started, shortly after the war. They are mainly 10-raters and 'A' boats, with a few Marbleheads and, more recently, 6-metres. There are also a few full size designs of various types and a couple of 'A' boats by W H Davey, the doyen of the Bournville club in the 1930s, and John's mentor when he was starting out as a designer.

Many of these plans were published in *Model Maker* and *Model Boats* and have been available over the years through the associated Plans Service; others were designs for private clients and have not been published previously. There is very little explanatory text and this is a book for those who enjoy plans for their own sake and who welcome the opportunity to have this important body of work conveniently collected in one place.

90   LUDBERG, Vilhelm Axelson:
Modellyachtsbyggnad: Stockholm, Wahlstrom &
Widstrand, 1923: 111, 8º.

We have not seen this, the only Swedish title on model yachting
that we have been able to locate.

*91   LEYLAND, Jane Anne: 'An 'A' Class Design
Development Program', a paper presented at *The
Ancient Interface XVII*, 1987: SNAME, 1987:
Typescript, 15, 25 cm.

Jane Leyland is a mathematician. In her youth she was a keen
model yacht skipper and designer. She and her mentor, Vic Ward,
jointly developed a series of 20 'A' Class designs over a period of 15
years. The series originated in the late 1940s and was originally
heavily influenced by the theories of Alfred Turner. *Beacon*, a boat
to his *Helios* design, played an important role in this development.

The paper recounts this development, with small but clear
lines drawings of each design and commentary on their
performance. In 1960 they won the MYRAA National
Championship with *Osi*.

92   McCANN, E Armitage: *Ship Model Making*: New
York, 1927.

We have not seen this. It may well be concerned only with scale
models as was the magazine of the period with which McCann was
associated.

*93   MACDONALD, D A: *Tuning Up a Model Yacht*:
Hemel Hempstead, Model and Allied Publications,
1957: 16, 8º.
Reprinted, London, The Curved Air Press,
(VMYG Reprints No 3) 1990:
ISBN: 1 873148 02 X: 16, 21cm.

This was originally part of a longer series on the building and
preparation of a competitive model, that appeared in *Model
Maker*. MacDonald, a member of the Clapham club, was one of the
leading skippers of the immediate post war era in Britain. It deals
with the techniques of setting up a new boat for free sailing
competition using vane gear.

*94   MARSHALL, Percival (ed): *Model Sailing Yachts,
How to Build Rig and Sail Them*: (*Model Engineer*
Hand Book No 4): London, Percival Marshall, n.d.,
but 1905 (Text by H Wilson THEOBALD): 114, 8°.
Reprinted (an almost entirely new text by
William John DANIELS): Marshall n.d., but
1913: 132, 8°.

Reprinted with additions 1919, 1921?, possibly
other dates before 1928.

New York, Spon and Chamberlain, 1919: [This
US edition is recorded by Toy, but seems to
have escaped both the National Union Catalog
and the NYPL Guide.]

2nd 'Revised' edition 1928 (Text by DANIELS):
London, Percival Marshall: 112, 8°.

Reprinted in the UK various times with minor
changes until 1950.

This little book has probably been the beginning of more model
yachting careers than any other.

The first edition, written by H Wilson Theobald, a young
barrister and member of the London MYC who had contributed
designs to the *Model Engineer*, is rare and contains his 1902
designs from *ME*, together with lines for a 5-rater and for a 36 foot
Linear Rater. His approach to construction is curious, involving
carving the 'bread and butter' hull in two halves, split down the
centre line. This may make cleaning out the inside easier, but it
involves hair raising methods of getting the two halves to go
together. Even as it appeared, most of its ideas and techniques
were being replaced by Bill Daniels' more advanced design
concepts, as evidenced in his 10-rater *XPDNC* .

Rather exceptionally for this sort of title, the publisher took
rapid action to bring his list up to date. Theobald had died in the
interim and Marshall turned to Daniels. Though still young, he
was already coming to occupy the dominant position he was to hold
in the sport for the remainder of his life. He produced a completely
new text and set of designs. The only part of the original that
survived (right up to the last printing in 1950) was the
introduction. This may have been written by Marshall himself.

Given that Marshall clearly recognised that Daniels was the
author he needed, it is surprising that he chose to keep his own

name on the cover and to make no acknowledgement of Daniels anywhere in the book itself. It was however clear to those in the sport that Daniels was the author.

The 1913 edition contains the 10-raters *XPDNC* and *Electra* and the schooner *Prospero*. The lines plans are very small, but are supplemented by tables of offsets. These designs represent some of the best of Daniels' pre-1914 output and they remained in print in this form right into the 1950s. This probably accounts for the large number of boats built to them over the years. The 1913 edition also has three 12-metre boats, *Yum, Substitute* and *Daphne*. In the immediate post war printings an 18 footer (Boat Racing Association) is added. Both this and the 12-metres disappear from the major revision of 1928, replaced by an 'A' boat *June*, (at this stage still called a YM6-m, despite its adoption as the International 'A' Class in 1927).

After this date the designs do not change except for the addition of a 36 Restricted Class design in the mid 1930s. Through the later printings the text shows only marginal alterations; the appendix listing Model Yachting Association affiliated clubs is sometimes updated, sometimes not.

95   MILLER, Thomas: *The Complete Modellist.*
Showing how to Raise the True and Exact model of any Ship or Vessel, Small or Great, either in Proportion or out of Proportion. Also the Manner to Find the Length of every Rope Exactly and Tables which give the true Bigness of every Rope in each Vessel. Together with the Weights of Anchors and Cables. Performed by Thomas Miller of great Yarmouth, Seaman: London, Printed by W G for George Hurlock, To be sold at his shop at St. Magnus Church, at the hither end of London Bridge, near Thames Street. 1667: iv, 20, 20cm.

We had hopes of including this as the oldest title on model making, by a distance. Alas, examination reveals that it is not about making models at all, but on the construction of accurate scale drawings of ships to facilitate the production of the right lengths of rope for the various parts of the standing and running rigging.

96   THE MODEL DOCKYARD: *The Model Dockyard Handy-Book*: London, The Model Dockyard, 1866. 4th edition, 1872: 76, 8º.

Reprint of 4th edition, with a new introduction by Russell POTTS: London, Curved Air Press (VMYG Reprint No 4), 1990: ISBN: 1 873148 03 8: vii, 38, oblong A4.

This is essentially the catalogue of a very superior model emporium. The Model Dockyard had been situated at 31 Fleet Street since the latter part of the 18th century, and prior to Bell's ownership, had been operated by Farley. Bell had taken over the business by 1861 and continued as 'model maker to the Admiralty' and to many inventors seeking to patent novel mechanical devices.

The tone of the extensive introductory matter is one of conscious superiority in the quality of his goods and of his socially eminent clientele, led by most of the Royal houses of Europe, and including the Prince Imperial of France. The author is equally sure that the steam engine represents the highest peak of human achievement and the commercial dominance of the British Empire the acme of civilisation.

The Dockyard offered a wide range of steam engine models, both as stationary demonstration devices for schools and colleges, or for the education of the children of the rich who were envisaged as his customers, and as power plants for a range of steamer models. They also offered locomotive models and associated model railway equipment.

There was a comprehensive range of castings from which the amateur could machine the parts to build his own steam engine and, exceptionally at such an early date, a smaller range of steam engines available as kits of finished parts, needing only a screwdriver to assemble.

The model yacht element of the catalogue included a wide range of models in all sizes from the impracticably small to the very impressively large. These were mainly of semi-scale style. Only one model is clearly aimed at competitive sailing and, despite the author's claim of close links with the model yachtsmen of the capital, there is no reference to any of the models being designed to Rating Rules in use by the various clubs then in existence. The General Rules and Sailing Regulations of the otherwise unknown 'Prince of Wales MYC', reported as sailing on the Serpentine, are reproduced and bear a close correspondence to those of the London MYC that sailed there in the 1850s.

The introduction to the reprint puts the Model Dockyard into its mid 19th century context.

Despite the long existence of the Model Dockyard and the heirloom quality of much of its more ambitious production, we know of no surviving model that can reliably be linked to this source.

We know of only two original copies of the *Handy-Book* in Britain, both of the 4th edition, though given that that edition claims to be the '21st Thousand', it is likely that other examples will be found somewhere. American library guides suggest that there are copies of the 2nd and 3rd editions in a library in Chicago. From the sheer extent of its production and assumed diffusion, the *Handy-Book* must have a significant place in the history of model engineering and of model yachting.

*97   **LE MODELE REDUIT DE BATEAU: *Construction et Pratique des Modèles de Bateaux*: 3rd Edition, Paris, Publications MRA, 1972: 25cm.**

The third edition of this title is the only one we have seen. It covers the construction techniques of model boats of all types.

The model yachting material covers construction, trimming and competition techniques for both free sailing and radio. The free sailing material is mainly concerned with Braine gears, which suggests that the material was written some time before the 1970s.

98   **THE MODERN BOY: *The Modern Boy's Book of Hobbies*: London, Percival Marshall, n. d., but 1937: 192, 4º.**

This is a glossy, well illustrated collection of articles covering a very wide range of activities. Despite the title, there appears to be no connection between it and its contemporary weekly *The Modern Boy*, published by Amalgamated Press. Amid the general run of popular technology topics for boys there are some very practical construction projects, including a number of model aircraft that are well up to date in both concept and construction technique.

There is also an article, 'Rig Your Yacht for Speed', which tells the reader how to replace the outdated gaff rig which it claims is still typical of commercial toy boats, with a more efficient bermuda rig, drawing on the latest aerodynamic information on the design of sail plans.

Though uncredited, the piece is clearly the work of a well informed model yachtsman, who is up to date with current practice in serious competitive sailing. Given Bill Daniels' longstanding links with Marshall, it is just possibly by him. It mentions Manfred

Curry's work on the aerodynamics of yacht sails and refers the reader to the 1928 English translation of his book.

The rig, sailmaking techniques and detailed arrangements proposed follow closely the best mainstream practice of the day, including the provision of a mast slide (in a simple form, made in wood) and an adjustable mast step. The instructions are sufficiently detailed to be of some value.

Surprisingly, in view of the advocacy of taller rigs, there is no discussion of the need to adjust the ballast to hold up a more powerful sail plan. Possibly the writer reckoned that the smaller sail area proposed would compensate, or that revising the ballast was too big a task for his schoolboy readers.

Possibly for similar reasons, the brief treatment of automatic steering discusses only weighted rudders, rather than the Braine gear used by serious model yachtsmen; it describes the use of two types widely found on commercial toys from the 1880s to the 1940s.

*99 **MOORE, Thomas:** *Build a Winning Model Yacht*: **New York, Fredk A Stokes, 1928: xi, 224, 8º.**

We have seen only photocopies of parts of this work. It gives a thorough treatment of design, as well as of construction and sailing. It contains several plans by Moore and others to the MYRAA Rules of the time, as well as 'A' boats by John Black (*Bostonia II*, the boat he took to England in 1927) and by J A Potter, (an unnamed design).

It reflects the US model yachting scene, as a group of clubs in the North East adjusted to US membership of IMYRA and the use of International class Rules. Those elsewhere, like the Washington group, of which Moore was a leading member, were slower to move away from the previous MYRAA classes. This impression of cultural lag may however be over-emphasised by Moore's using designs that he had prepared for publication earlier to accompany his articles in the journals of the day

100 **MUSCIANO, Walter A:** *Building and Operating Model Ships*: **New York, Funk and Wagnall, 1965.**

We have not seen this. It may be something very similar to the following entry, which dates from the same year.

101 **MUSCIANO, Walter A:** *Building and Sailing Model Boats*: **New York, McBride, 1965: 190, 4º.** **British edition, (revised by Ron G MOULTON): London, Robert Hale, 1976: 190, 4º.**

The text of the British edition, which is the only one we have seen, is entirely given over to power models, most of them fairly simple.

Many of the illustrations are of much more sophisticated models than those treated in the text. There are appendices of contact addresses for Model Power Boat Association clubs and, strangely, for the member nations of the International Model Yacht Racing Union. The final appendix purports to be a list of Model Yacht Association affiliated clubs, but contains only 10 of the 50-60 then in existence. These two appendices are the only acknowledgement of model sailing activity.

102   NEWNES: *Model Boat Building (Newnes' Home Mechanics Books)*: London, George Newnes Ltd, 1931: 96, 8°.

One of a series of titles, mainly on more practical matters such as home electric appliances, but including this and a volume on toy making. Some of the others in the series are credited to individual authors, usually **F J Camm**, who was a contributor to and later editor of *Home Mechanics*. This volume is clearly the work of several hands, and deals with a range of simple powered models, as well as a toy sailing boat and a number of chapters on model yachting. These last are almost certainly by Camm. The exact relationship of this work to Camm's later book of the same title (No. 19) is unclear.

Though there are four substantial chapters on aspects of model yachting, they do not form a coherent whole and contain nothing on construction as such, and no designs. Throughout the author conducts a bad tempered argument with straw men, characterised as 'supposed experts'.[8] The material on sails and rigging is old fashioned for its date and the discussion of rating Rules is ill-informed and very unhelpful to a novice reader. The diagrams in the section on sail planning are identical to those that appear in Camm's *Model Boat Building*.

We can only assume that these were parts of Camm's writing on model yachts that had appeared in the magazine and were hoist into this collection to fill up the necessary number of pages.

103   NORDNER, W: *How to Build Model Ships*: Des Moines, IA, Meredith, 1970.

We have not seen this; we are told that only a few pages refer to sailing models.

---

[8] Camm seems to have managed to fall out with the authorities in most fields. His writing on aeromodelling is spotted with captious criticism of the SMAE and the way it chooses to conduct its competitions.

104   *OXFORD CHILDREN'S ENCYCLOPAEDIA*:
         Oxford, OUP, 1973.

The brief entry on 'models' includes some treatment of model yachts. A few sentences on the history of the sport, an explanation of the reasons why scale models of full size craft are less effective than boats designed as models and on the development of modern sail plans. The operation of vane gear is described and drawn. There is also reference to the use of radio control, to the classes sailed and the role of the MYA as National Authority. A good coverage within its very tight space limit.

105   **POPULAR SCIENCE MONTHLY:** *Manual of Ship Model Making. Where are Clearly Explained and Diagrammed many Short Cuts, Kinks and Time Saving Methods...etc*: **New York, Popular Science Publishing, 1934: 192, 8°.**
         Reprinted, 1935, 1938.

One chapter in this compendium discusses 'Model Yacht Racing' and offers instruction in the construction of a scale model of the 1930s J Class yacht *Enterprise*.

*106   **PÖRSCHMANN, Otto Peter:** *Von Schiffen und vom Schiffsmodellbau*: **Berlin, Verlag Neues Leben, 1954.**

This title, published in the DDR, is valuable for its detailing of the rating Rules as used there. As well as the international A, 6-metre and Marblehead classes, there are full texts of the German C, E, F and G class rules. We have seen only this section, but we understand that the book includes treatment of construction and sailing techniques. In 1954 the Marblehead Rule, as used in the DDR, included a requirement that the area of the vane feather, if used, should be included in the sail area calculation.

*107   **POTTS, Russell:** *100 Years of the 10-Rater Rule*: **Goteburg, SMSF, 1987: 18, 21cm.**
         2nd edition: London, Curved Air Press, 1990: ISBN 1 873148 05 4: 18, 21cm

This brief history of design development under the Length and Sail Area Rule was prepared as a souvenir for the Radio 10-rater World Championships in Sweden in 1987, which marked the Centenary of the Rule. It covers the development of the free sailing 10-rater in the UK from its adoption by modellers in the 1880s to 1987. It is illustrated with many lines plans and photos, but contains no discussion of the rather different development of the 10-rater under radio control.

108   POTTS, Russell: 'Sporting Hobbies and Social Class: the case of Model Yachting', in *The International Journal of Sports History*, 5, (1988), 206-233.

This is the first serious academic work on the history of model yachting. It discusses the social background of 19th century modellers and two episodes of social conflict involving London clubs sailing in the Royal Parks.

109   POTTS, Russell: *'M' 1930-1990, A Design History of the Marblehead Class of Model Yacht*: London, Curved Air Press, 1990: 1 873148 04 6: 24, 21cm.

This was a souvenir publication for the 1990 World Championships held at Fleetwood. It covers the history of the class from its introduction in the USA to its present world wide diffusion and discusses how the shape of the boats has changed and why. Unlike the 10-rater title (No 107), it covers the introduction of radio control and its effect on the design and construction of boats. It is profusely illustrated with lines drawings.

110   POTTS, Russell : 'The 6-metre Class: its Origins and Development' in *Wavelengths, the Newsletter of the 6-Metre Owners Association*, May and September, 1993.

This was the beginning of an uncompleted series of articles, that petered out after dealing with the model and full size designs to the predecessor Linear Rating Rules of 1896 and 1901. A more extended treatment of some of the issues affecting full size design is included in the following item.

111   POTTS, Russell: *The Social Construction of a Leisure Technology: Yacht Design and the Rating Rules, 1880-1920*: London, The Curved Air Press, 1995: 70, 25cm.

This is the text of an M.Sc. dissertation. It is not directly concerned with model yachts, but is a study of the interplay of technical and non-technical factors influencing design and the way these operate through continuing debate over the form of the Rating Rule to be used. Illustrated with many lines plans of full size yachts of the period.

112   POZZINI, Charles L, and Earl O PHILLIPS: *How to Build and Sail a Model Yacht*: Bloomington, IL, McKnight and McKnight, 1968: 88.

We have not seen this. It is a late example of the school shop programme text, written by a pair of manual arts teachers. It contains plans and instructions for the 'Detroit 24', which is still used in what is apparently the last surviving regular school district regatta in the USA.

*113   PREUSS, Herbert: *Der Schiffsmodellbau in der deutschen Schule. (Wehrgeistige Erziehung zur Kriegsmarine, Heft 8)*: Berlin, E S Mittler und Sohn, 1943: 156, 8⁰.

Written by a serving naval officer and published with the authority of the German Navy's 'central establishment for ship modelling', this was, apparently, only one of a series of volumes intended to contribute to the inculcation of the military spirit in schools on behalf of the Navy.

After introductory chapters on 'the significance of ship modelling in schools' and on 'ways of fostering maritime awareness through craft lessons', the author gets down to some serious discussion of sailing boats and the physics of sailing, illustrated by wind tunnel flow diagrams and parallelograms of forces. We have not seen the chapters on construction, but there appears to be comprehensive coverage of all the standard methods, with separate chapters on spars, rig and sailing techniques. There is some treatment of scale models of naval and merchant vessels, but this is a very much a subsidiary topic. Space is also given to the rating and competition rules for model yachting.

Overall, this is a book that is essentially about model yachts, with a little extraneous matter thrown in; so far as we can judge a competent and up to date textbook for its period. The only question that remains is how, in 1943, the German war machine could justify the diversion of even this much effort to teaching schoolboys how to play with toy boats. It offers an oblique perspective on the relative failure of a totalitarian state realistically to mobilise its efforts for the job in hand.

114   PRICE, Brick: *The Model Shipbuilding Handbook*: USA, 1983.

We have not seen this. It may have no sailing model content as the author's other published work is a series of motorcycle maintenance manuals, which suggests that his model interests may be in power boats.

*115   PRIEST, B Hamilton & John A LEWIS: *Model Racing Yachts. Their Architecture, Design, Construction and Handling*: Hemel Hempstead, MAP, n.d., but 1966: 112, 4⁰.

Despite being over 30 years old, this is still the most recent comprehensive treatment of model yacht design and draws on the experience of two of the most successful designers of the 1950s and

60s. Though the designs it contains are now outdated, the discussion of the design process is as good as it ever was, with the proviso that there is no discussion of the rather freer procedures that became possible with the introduction of the fin and bulb concept.

There is detailed discussion of the 'A', 'M' and 10-rater Classes and a brief history of design developments in the 'A' Class. The section on trimming and sailing is valuable and throws an interesting light on the methodical practice of Dick Priest. There is brief treatment of construction, with some fittings drawings, including a vane gear design.

The lines plans included are of ample size and include the 'A' boats *Top Hat, Commando, Saxon, Highlander* and *Moonshine*, the 10-r *Whirlwind* and the 'M's *Witchcraft, Witch* and *Bewitched*. Dick Priest died some years ago, but John Lewis is still active as a designer. (See No. 89)

116   RANDIER, Jean: *L'Objet de Marine*: Paris,
Gallimard, 1992: ISBN: 2 07 060267 2: 182, large 4°.
We have not seen this and the material is supplied by one of our informants.

It is a large format 'coffee table' book devoted to maritime collectibles of all kinds. It contains many fine photographs of beautiful objects. The text is a survey of the fine and folk arts associated with the sea and seafaring, covering the full range of paintings, uniforms, instruments, figureheads and the like. Models are fully covered, including scale models, half models, ships in bottles, tin toy boats, live steam and sailing pond models.

The brief chapter on pond models, or as the French refer to them, 'yachting models', covers the full range from commercial toys to very serious 'A' class racers. The author draws the proper distinctions between pleasure and racing models, between free and radio controlled sailing and between one-off and class models. There are illustrations of sailing models covering a span from the 1880s to the 1960s, which draw attention to the compromises necessary between scale like representation and practical sailing performance. There is some discussion of the Rating Rules that control racing models and of the Racing Rules that control competition.

The author is aware that not all models intended to sail did so successfully, and that some never reached the water.

*117   REECE, Trevor: *Radio Control Model Yachts*:
            Hemel Hempstead, Argus, 1989:
            ISBN: 0 85252 972 X: 175, 25cm.
            as *Modellyachten ferngesteuert*: Villingen-
            Schwenningen, Neckar-Verlag, 1992:
            ISBN 3 88181 042 5: 216, 23cm.

This is a book on the current style of radio controlled yacht racing and its commercially available vehicles. It gives a lot of space to the installation of radio and to the trimming and adjustment sails but its constructional matter is limited to a single chapter on the construction of GRP kits and one, of only eight pages, on building planked hulls in wood. This in itself is a reflection of the change in the nature of model yachting since radio came to dominate the sport. Because there is no treatment of design and next to none of construction from scratch, there are no lines plans. Sailmaking is also absent.

Though there is a lot of useful information in the text, the organisation makes it hard to find. There are good explanatory drawings and some good photos, but a disappointing book, which could have been a lot better.

118   REEVES, W Bernard: *How to Make a High Class
            Fast Sailing Yacht Model. A New Quick and Easy
            Method of Construction; a £5.5s Yacht for Five
            Shillings*: London, Modelcraft, 1943: 18, 4º.
            2nd edition, 1944: 18, 4º.

Reeves was a naval architect, who also wrote more extensively about scale ship modelling. The design proposed here is for a 24 inch, near symmetrical, circular arc hull, to be constructed in two layers of strawboard planks. These were to be glued with fish glue treated with bichromate of potash and ironed to a waterproof and highly finished state over a skeleton jig. The design is in other respects conventional, as is the sail plan and the Braine steering gear.

A personal note.

This is a book close to my heart as I owned a copy as a boy of 11 and my first, failed, attempt to build a boat was to the design and using the system proposed in it. No doubt the use of strawboard was to get round the wartime shortage of wood, but I imagine many boys and their mothers were reduced to the same tears **of** frustration as it comprehensively refused to go together in the way described.

In my egoistic way, I had assumed that, if I had failed, no one else could have succeeded and that the enthusiastic endorsement by a builder that appears in the second edition was a work of fiction. A few years ago, however, I was given a boat built from this book at the time it appeared. It had all the bumps and lumps one might expect and is seriously overweight from the quantities of glue and paint that have gone into it. Despite restoration and waterproofing by methods not available to Reeves, I have not yet dared to put it on the water. **RP**

The book was still in print in the late 1950s.

*119   RIES, Freidrich Karl: *RC Yachtbau-Praxis: Marblehead-Klasse*: Villingen-Schwenningen, Neckar-Verlag, 1976: ISBN 3 7883 0121 X: 80, 21cm.

*120   RIES, Freidrich Karl: *Bau Vörschläge für M-Boote*: Villingen-Schwenningen, Neckar-Verlag, (SchiffsModell Spezial) 1982: ISBN 3 7883 0199 6: 64, 24cm.

*121   RIES, Freidrich Karl: *Modellyachtbau-Praxis, mit Bauplan fur 'C88 II' im 1 : 1 maßtab*: Villingen-Schwenningen, Neckar-Verlag, (Schiffsmodell Fach Buch)1989: ISBN 3 7883 1121 5: 64, 24cm.

*122   RIES, Freidrich Karl: *Marblehead-Boote: Entwicklung einer Segelklasse*: Villingen-Schwenningen, Neckar-Verlag, (Modell Fachbuch) 1982: ISBN 3 7883 0179: 128, 24cm.

We have seen only parts of one of these titles, issued by the publishers of the magazine *SchiffsModell*. As they are written by a well known German skipper, designer and supplier of kits and equipment, who was a regular contributor to the magazine, they will deal with current practice for competitive radio yachts. One at least contains full size construction drawings; almost certainly these will be for a Marblehead class yacht.

The last title, of which we have seen a few pages, deals with some aspects of the theory underlying the development of a Marblehead design before getting on with the process of construction. Much of it is concerned with the building of a GRP kit for *Anja XIV*, a very successful design by the Swiss skipper Lupart, for which Ries was the commercial distributor. It is essentially an extended instruction booklet for the kit.

*123   **RIES, Freidrich Karl:** *Bau von fernegesteurung Modellyacht der M-Klasse*: **No location, Verlag fur Technik und Handwerk, 1993: 80, 23 cm.**
We have not seen this title, which appears to be another treatment of the building of a modern radio controlled Marblehead.

124   **RIGBY, Wallis:** *Making Model Ships*: **London, Ward Lock, 1957: 80, 8º.**
Though this appears in the bibliographical sources, we have not been able to locate a copy. Rigby wrote a similar title on model aircraft in the 1930s.

125   **ROIG, Juan Miguel:** *Vocabulario Inglés-Castellano de Terminos Usados en Yatemodelismo*: **Buenos Aires, Club Argentino de Yatemodelismo, 1998: 34, 21 cm.**
Juan Roig has acted as team manager for at least two Argentine entries to world championships and is also the editor of CAYM's journal *Buenas Amuras*. This brief specialist dictionary is designed to assist Spanish speaking skippers when competing in an English speaking environment. As well as a comprehensive technical dictionary, it includes a phrase book appendix of the terms most frequently needed in actual competition, complete with a pronunciation guide, a bi-lingual list of abbreviations and a guide to numbers and their pronunciation.

*126   **ROBINSON, Larry and Bob WELLS:** *Optimising the East Coast 12-meter*: **Mercer Island, WA, Ragged Symmetry Publications, 1997: 240, 27 cm.**
This is an extension of **Bob WELLS'** earlier book (No. 154) and a more technical treatment of the preparation and trimming of the EC 12-m for peak performance. It draws on a great deal of development work done, particularly by Larry, over the years 1989-96 and depicts and describes in detail two leading boats in the class, one of them that of Kelly Martin, many times US National Champion. Though written in the context of this one design class, where extracting the last ounce of performance by altering those parts of the system amenable to change under the Rules is critical in a competitive fleet, much of the material and techniques are applicable to improving the performance of any radio controlled racing model.

*127   ROBINSON, Larry: *Making Model Yacht Sails*:
Mercer Island, WA, Ragged Symmetry
Publications, 1998: 89, 27 cm.

A series of articles on the construction of panelled sails from modern film materials, with meticulous attention paid to the definition and control of sail camber. Larry has developed methods of production using precision shaped sail blocks that allow close and repeatable control of panel seams, and thus of sail camber. Part 2 explains with pictures how to reinforce the panelled sail blank with 'strings' of flexible fibres that lie along the load paths in the sail. One major advantage claimed is the ability to preserve sail camber at the head of the sail. Immensely labour intensive, but convincingly described and probably the way we shall all have to go to go for light weather sails. Amid the detailed description of methods there is much thoughtful comment on wider issues of sail construction and trim.

This is a lovely example of the application of intelligence and hard work to the development of a satisfying technological solution.

128   SCHOETTLE Edwin J, (ed): *Sailing Craft*: New
York, Macmillan, 1928: xii, 728, 4°.

This large collection is devoted almost exclusively to full size sailing and consists mainly of short essays on an enormous variety of yacht types and classes. Some of these are of national and international importance; many are local one design classes. There are some historical pieces and some treatment of design considerations and current research into sail aerodynamics. Overall it gives, as was intended, a good conspectus of North American pleasure sailing at the end of the 1920s.

It contains one contribution on model yachts, by **Charles Z CLAUDER**, an architect and amateur model builder. It deals only with the building of scale models of full size craft, typically at about 36 inch lwl. He discusses these only fairly superficially, apart from some treatment of the scaling problems of building practical small replicas, for which his solution is 'to lower the centre of gravity'. This he achieves by building the model almost entirely in balsa wood, and transferring the weight saved in the structure to the ballast. Even the mast was made from balsa, 'wrapped with four layers of stout paper' to provide additional strength. There is some discussion of Froude's work on size and speed relationships, but nothing else of interest.

The editor was clearly unhappy with this rather scrappy contribution and weighed in with a supplementary note on the only model experiments he could call to mind. He reproduces Franklin's 1768 letter on his model tests on the effect of the depth of water on the resistance generated by barges being towed in a canal. Fascinating, but irrelevant to our purpose.

*129   SKENE, Norman Locke: *Elements of Naval Architecture*: Fifth edition, New York, The Rudder. 1935. London, John Lane, the Bodley Head, 1936: ix, 244, 4º.
Sixth edition, (re-written by George F CROUCH): New York, Dodd Mead, 1938. London, A & C Black, 1948: ix, 252, 4º.

This standard work on the naval architecture of yachts and small power boats was first published in the USA in 1902 by *The Rudder*. In its original form it was concerned solely with full size practice. but it went through progressive revisions, and by the time of the fifth edition, but possibly earlier, it contained a final chapter on model yachts. Skene was a member of the Boston MYC in the 1920s and 30s.

In the fifth edition, this chapter treats very briefly of the use of models as ornament and as aids in the design process, commenting, (before Davidson's work for *Ranger* in the tank at the Stevens Institute), that

> ... it is not possible to learn much from [tank] testing sailing models, as the effect of the wind on flotation, balance and trim is pretty complex.

Most of the text is devoted to discussion of serious model yachting from the designer's point of view, emphasising that he has to make a very different disposition of the elements of a rating formula for a model than he would for full size craft.

There are nomograph tables showing the trade-offs between the leading characteristics of models designed to the MYRAA Class B, the YM 6-metre, (which was to become the International 'A' class) and the MYRAA R Class. The photo illustrations are drawn almost entirely from the racing at Gosport in the 1927 competition for the *Yachting Monthly* Cup, and were presumably supplied by John Black, the Boston MYC member who represented the US on that occasion.

The following edition retains most of the peripheral material and the nomographs unchanged, but substantially revises the text to reduce the space given to MYRAA classes and increase the discussion of the 'A' Class, including the complete text of the Rule. His assessment of the typical size of an 'A' boat is revised upwards to reflect the design developments in the interim.

There is also some discussion of the newly introduced Marblehead class, on which he comments that 'the 'M' is easier to build (he means design) than an 'A' boat, but that 'the class contains some freaks'. The photo illustrations are updated to the 1937 *YM* Cup competition.

Subsequent editions are revised and substantially rewritten by Kinney and the model yachting material disappears.

*130   SMEED, Victor Ernest: *Boat Modelling*: Hemel Hempstead, MAP, 1956: 128, 4⁰.

15 reprints to 1977.

2nd, revised edition, Hemel Hempstead, Argus, 1985: ISBN 0 85242 848 0: 128, 21cm.

reprinted several times.

This book played much the same part in model boating in the 1950s as the **Percival Marshall** title (No. 95) did in the inter-war years. Constantly reprinted over the years and covering both powered and sailing models, it must have been the starting point for very many entrants to the sport. Given the wide range of its coverage, the amount of strictly model yachting material it contains is limited. Even so, it has lot of sound information on how to build a first model that will work. Lots of useful drawings of fittings and ways of doing things, but no lines plans

131   SMEED, Victor Ernest (ed.): *The Model Maker Manual*: Watford, MAP, 1957: 128, 21cm.

This is a compendium covering the whole range of topics appropriate to the readership of the magazine *Model Maker* in the 1950s; most of the items could equally well have appeared in the monthly sequence. The model yachting element includes 10-rater designs by **John Lewis** and a round up of designs from Russia and Yugoslavia. The Russian drawings, for an 'M' and a 10-rater, are conventional, even outdated, but the Yugoslav design, to the NAVIGA 1-metre Rule, is extremely sophisticated, with an early form of swing rig (though with an overlapping headsail that would not self tack), a revolving mast and a hull design intended to reduce wind resistance.

132   SMEED, Victor Ernest: *Simple Model Yachts*: Hemel Hempstead, MAP, 1965.

A short pamphlet, with three small and easy to build projects for beginners. The most elaborate is a small semi-scale cruiser to be built by bread and butter methods in balsa.

*133   SMEED, Victor Ernest: *Model Yachting*:
Rickmansworth, Smeed 1977: 122, 21cm.
Reprinted: Hemel Hempstead, Argus, 1984:
ISBN 0 90816 200 9: 122, 21cm.

When Vic retired from the editorship of **Model Boats** to free-lance,
he set out to write down what he knew about model yachting. As he
must have forgotten more than most of us ever knew, there is a lot
of good stuff here. There is very little discussion of design and no
lines plans, but profuse illustrations of fittings and devices of all
kinds. Some of the ideas are now a bit outdated, and may have
been so even when first published, but much of value.

134   SMEED, Victor Ernest: *The World of Model Ships*:
London, Paul Hamlyn, 1979: ISBN: 0 600 38420 9:
192, 4º.

A general survey of the entire field of marine modelling. The
information on each aspect of the hobby is necessarily at a fairly
basic level. If anything, model yachting gets more than its fair
share of both text and illustration. There is some coverage of
construction and rigging methods, but too brief to be very helpful.
The lavish photo illustrations give a good impression of the model
yachting scene in Britain in the 1970s.

135   SMITH, Bernard: *The 40-Knot Sailboat*: New York,
Grosset & Dunlap, London, Harrap, 1963: 140, 4º.

This is not strictly a model yachting book, but tells the story of a
series of model experiments spread over a long period, to develop a
novel type of foil borne sailing vessel, potentially capable of high
speeds. It is beautifully presented and starts from a consideration
of the basic problems of the sail powered vessel and contains a
much compressed history of the development of sailing vessels,
before getting down to describing the development of his own ideas
and their embodiment in a series of models.

There is also, for those that want it, full technical and
theoretical treatment of the design considerations underlying his
approach. Most of this work pre-dates that of Grogogno and others
on foil borne craft, as well as the designs developed for the speed
competitions held at in the UK at Portland in the 1970s and 80s.

Smith was a guided weapons engineer and eventually head of
the US Navy's Bureau of Weapons. As a leisure activity, he
developed small free sailing models of wind powered hydrofoil craft.
These progressed from extremely crude to extremely sophisticated,
using surface piercing foils of substantial volume, able to support
the weight of the vessel at rest, and a solid aerofoil.

Apart from the increasing ingenuity of his construction, his major innovation was the use of an asymmetrical, proa, configuration, with the vessel supported on only two foils and a third, 'reversed' foil used as a stabiliser. This was set to windward and held the craft down by hydrodynamic forces. His only full size example was relatively early in the sequence and was neither as sophisticated nor as successful as his later model versions. His final design for a man-carrying version of his 'aero-hydrofoil' was, so far as we know, never realised and, for all its ingenious engineering, would probably have had difficulty in matching the speeds achieved by much simpler, specially developed sailboards.

*136 **STANSFIELD-HICKS, C:** *Yachts, Boats and Canoes, with Special Chapters on Model Yachts and Single-handed Sailing*: **London, Sampson, Low, Marston, Searle & Rivington , New York, Forest and Stream, 1887: xi, 384, 8º.**
As *Jachten, Boote und Kanoes*: **Leipzig, Hirt und Sohn, 1888: 316, 8º.**

Stansfield-Hicks was a lifelong model yachtsman and sailor of small single handed boats. His book, written when he was relatively young, (he did not die until the 1930s) is, despite its title, very largely taken up with model yachting. At least half the text deals with models rather than the canoes and small yachts of the title.

It is, for so early a book, sophisticated in its design concepts and is probably the most advanced treatment of the theory of yacht design then available, not excluding Dixon Kemp's *Yacht Designing*. It devotes considerable space to discussing the styles of yacht produced by particular rating rules, as well as emphasising the importance of the diagonals in determining the fairness of a design. He recognises that Scott Russell's wave line theory is flawed and shows how Froude's work, with which he is fully familiar, had influenced design of both models and full size craft.

He believes, however, that even in Tonnage Rule models, too enthusiastic an effort to reduce wetted area by rounding up the forefoot can be detrimental to the steadiness of a model's course, and thus to her overall performance. He also believes that models need a more upright stern post than full size craft and a proportion of true deadwood aft to promote steadiness of tracking. This is typical of the concern of modellers for steadiness of course over absolute speed.

Like most writers on the subject he claims that 'the present advanced type' of model yachting, '... is of comparatively recent date'. He also remarks on what he sees as the classless nature of model yachting 'in which all classes of society may engage in courteous rivalry and the man of high attainments compete with the artisan'. This was perhaps an over optimistic assessment of the extent to which Victorian concepts of social propriety could be overcome by a common enthusiasm, but reflects both the broad attraction of the sport and his own philanthropic motivation. In later life he was active in charity work among destitute youths in the East End.

There is an extended discussion of the problem of models 'running off' when pressed hard, with several practical, and some less practical, ideas on how it might be cured. Even so well informed a writer has no concept that even approximates to the calculated hull balance that was to solve the problem a further thirty years on.

Complete chapters on model sail design and construction and on spars and rigging give a good conspectus of the most advanced practice of the day, as does the chapter on sailing techniques for models. The hull construction advocated is bread and butter, in a rather heavy style with hull walls of ¼ inch thickness for a 36 inch model and bosses left in the lifts so that they may be screwed together.

There is a good collection of plans of decent size at the end. Five of these are for models, four of which come from the Liverpool MYC and are to the '1730' Tonnage Rule. The one exception is a Length Rule boat from Hull, designed by T A Bruce; this must have been of somewhat earlier date than the book, since the Kingston club, with Liverpool, was one of the first to adopt the '1730' Rule. The plans are supplemented by valuable information on the performance and success or otherwise of boats built to them.

An appendix gives the complete text of the sailing Rules used at Liverpool. These show that though the models were measured by the '1730' Rule, the club imposed a number of additional local clauses. These set out to restrict the depth of the hull and to enforce a minimum freeboard, the use of bulwarks of a specified height, a counter and a rig that bore a resemblance to that of a full size yacht of similar type. Clearly, they did not wish their models to deviate from what they though of as 'proper' yacht-like style, even in pursuit of superior performance.

This concern to control some aspects of the model design, even though the full size Rule does not do so, is also found at South Shields at the same period and may have been the practice elsewhere. Details of club Rules have not so far come to light from other localities.

137   STORCH. K: *Die Modelljacht. Eine Anleitung zum Selbstbauen von Boot- und Jachtmodellen und Kanoes*: Berlin, Albrecht Dürer-haus, n.d. but 1910: iv, 25, 8°.

This is not a substantial work, but interesting in that it is the product of teacher in the Royal Art Academy of Königsberg. The model yachting material occupies at least two thirds of the space and gives brief instructions on the construction of simple yacht models by the bread and butter method. It is the first of a long line of books in German intended for use in school craft classes and the illustrations show schoolboys at work at the bench. There are plans for a number of sailing models. We have seen only those for an 80cm semi-scale cutter, and for an open, clinker planked, dinghy. Both of these are noted as being too advanced for school use, but we have not seen the presumably simpler designs that Storch recommends for this purpose.

*138   TILLER, Arthur: *Die Modell-Yacht: Konstruktion, Bau und Segeln von Modell-Yachten. Mit 100 Skizzen, 2 Tafeln und 7 Konstruktionszeichungen*: Berlin, Wedekind, (Yacht-Bibliothek, Band V), 1911 (on title; 1910 on reverse title): viii, 106, 4°.

Tiller (1884-1957) was a naval architect who published on model yachting and, to a lesser extent, on other water based sports from 1911 to 1955. His output included a series of model designs, each in a folder with building instructions, published during the 1939-45 war as part of the long *Spiel und Arbeit* series of the Ravensburg house of Maier. These designs are to a series of classes established by the *Deutscher Seglerverband* in the 1930s and adopted also by the marine section of the *Hitlerjugend*.

He was a major force in German model yachting in the inter-war period and is noted as the designer of at least two 'A' boats for planned but ultimately aborted challenges for the *Yachting Monthly* Cup. Much of his writing is aimed a good deal lower and is clearly intended for beginners and juniors. He was a cosmopolitan figure, working in Scandinavia in the early 1920s and travelling to the USA and to Argentina after 1945. A Spanish translation of one of his titles on full size sailing was published in Buenos Aires as late as 1955. He had returned to Germany by the time of his death.

This, his earliest model yachting title, was published as part of a good technical library associated with Wedekind's magazine for full size sailors, *Die Yacht*. Copies are relatively rare. In the preface, Tiller contrasts what he claims is a high level of activity among German model yachtsmen with the paucity of writing on the subject. He seems to claim priority in writing on model yachting in

German, but may not have been aware of Storch's work, (No. 136), that appeared in the same year.

It is clearly a naval architect's book. It starts off with discussion of the various rating Rules used in German clubs, the types of design that these produced and the effects on design of serious competition, with special reference to the 5 Kg. displacement class of the Kiel club, with which he is clearly intimately familiar.

There follows a thoughtful discussion of the design process, that draws equally as much on his full size practice as on model experience. The construction techniques suggested are for plank-on-frame models, fairly closely paralleling full size methods, and perhaps a little heavier than necessary for model purposes. Some suggested weight tables give only a 49% ballast ratio for a 6 Kg. model using sawn frames and 52% for a 5 Kg. model built with bent frames. There is also description of triple diagonal planking in veneer. The design of spars, fittings and the like is over complex and follows full size practice more closely than is really necessary.

The section on sailing technique is competent and includes diagrams of automatic steering devices that first appeared in Fisher's articles in *Rudder*.

Seven designs are included, mainly for the displacement classes, including some that are only there to show what, in Tiller's view, was the wrong way to approach the problem.

*139   TILLER, Arthur: *Modellyachtbau und Segeln. Zweite, völlig umgearbeitete und vermehrte Auflage von 'Die Modell-Yacht'. Konstruktion, Bau und Segeln von Modellsegel-Yachten. Mit über 200 abbildungen und vielen konstruktionstafln von ausgeführten Modellsegel-Yachten*: Berlin, Wedekind, (Yacht-Bibliothek Band XV) 1922: vi, 231, 4º.
Reprint, Berlin, Delius, Klasing, 1926.

This second version of Tiller's serious work on model yachting again appeared originally in the *Die Yacht* library. It is much expanded and reorganised but, despite this and its change of title, is clearly regarded by Tiller as a second edition rather than a new work. The foreword is signed from Copenhagen.

The expanded discussion of measurement Rules follows much the same path as in the 1911 title, but is more scathing about the distortions produced by the displacement Rules used in Kiel and Hamburg. The discussion of design procedures is little different, though the treatment of sail plans includes some new material on the aerodynamics of sails and the need for controlling the shape of the sail.

The construction section is much expanded to include bread and butter techniques (both on the waterlines and on the buttocks) and hard chine construction. There is also more detail on the casting of lead, the fitting of rudders and the like. The plank-on-frame section remains as in 1911, except for a backward looking section incorporating ideas and drawings taken, without acknowledgement, from **Grosvenor** (No. 54).

The sailing techniques element is essentially the same, but with a wider range of automatic steering gear designs, including a whole series of drawings taken from H H Simpson's articles in *Yachting Monthly*. A chapter is given over to the design and construction of a skiff suitable for handling model yachts. This reflects the practice of the Hamburg and Kiel clubs, and possibly others in Germany.

The plans supplement is expanded. Three designs are carried forward from 1911. Many of the new ones still date from before 1914 and include much larger yachts than in the earlier version. The displacement classes run up to 50 Kg., and there are as well designs to the (English) Linear Rating Rule of 1901 and to the International (Metre) Rule of 1906. All these designs show heavy 'scale' influences in both hull and rig and some are rigged as schooners, possibly in imitation of the large full size schooner yachts designed by Oertz for the Kaiser and Krupp.

Tiller also includes a number of designs drawn from British and French sources, some of which we have not seen elsewhere. For instance, he has the only lines drawing we have seen for the late, decadent, style of 10 Tonner to the '1730' Rule sailed in the North East of England early in this century. This example is by A Long, a noted skipper of the day and a draughtsman in a Tyneside shipyard. Apart from a small number of more recent designs, all by Tiller himself and dated 1920 and 1921, there is little in the second edition that is obviously up to date and could not have appeared in 1911.

Tiller was well read in the foreign literature of the sport and had no qualms about taking designs and other material from wherever he found them. After this very comprehensive and serious title, the rest of his output is significantly less elevated.

140   TILLER, Arthur: *Modell-Segel-Yachten*:
              Ravensburg, Maier, (Spiel und Arbeit No 114)
              1929: 68, 8º.
              Reprinted 1939, 1952.

We have not seen this title, which if it was reprinted without
alteration in 1952, must have been seriously out of date. The Maier
list shows it as 'Part I' and concerned with carved hulls. See the
following item.

Maier's *Spiel und Arbeit* series originated in 1900 with a
design for a 65 cm. model yacht, but covered an immense range of
other modelling and constructional projects. Within the total
production, model boats are only a very small part.

141   TILLER, Arthur: *Modell-Segel-Yachten*:
              Ravensburg, Maier, (Spiel und Arbeit No 141)
              1933: 68, 8º.

This is 'Part II' and deals with planked hulls. We have not seen it,
and there is no record of its having been reprinted, but Maier's lists
show it as still available in 1943.

142   TILLER. Artur: *Modellsegelboote fur Angefänger*:
              Ravensburg, Maier, (Spiel und Arbeit No 161)
              1936: 24, 8º.
              Reprinted 1943, 1949.

We have not seen this. It appears to be a brief introduction for
beginners. From this date Tiller chooses to use a more 'deutsch'
spelling of his forename. Similarly, subsequent titles choose to spell
'jacht' with a 'j'.

*143   TILLER, Artur: *Modelljachtbau, das Werkbuch der
              bewährten Bauweisen*: Ravensburg, Maier, 1938.
              Reprinted, 1940, 1951.

This is a much simpler book than the 1911 or 1921 titles and has
no design discussion. We have seen only the 1951 printing, which
may differ in some respects from the earlier versions. There is a
supplement that contains small reproductions of a number of
Tiller's designs from the inter-war and war time period.

The construction material is not significantly different from
that in his earlier works and must have seemed out of date to
readers with more than a superficial knowledge of current practice.
The tone and intended market are probably best indicated by the
dust wrapper, which has photos of young boys, sailing small and
simple models.

*144   TILLER, Artur: *Das Segln von Modelljachten; Eine Einfuhrung in der automatische Steuring fur Angfänger und Fortegeschrittene. Klassen- und Wettesgelbestimmungen der Modellsegelabteilung des Deutschen Segler-Verbandes*: Berlin, Matthiesen, 1941: 96, 8°.
Second, 'corrected' edition: 1944.

We have not seen all of this work. It appears to be devoted to the sailing rather than the design and construction of model yachts. There is a substantial section on the history of automatic steering gears, that covers most of the devices from the weighted rudder to the most sophisticated forms of Braine gear, with jib steering. Considering its date of publication, it is curiously old fashioned, making no mention of vane gears and relying on foreign publications from the early part of the century for its technical illustrations. Possibly it was a war time pot boiler for Tiller.

145   TUTTLE, E W: *How to Make and Sail a Model Yacht*: Elizabeth NJ, Practical Arts, n. d., (1930s)

We have not seen this. It appears to be another example of the 'how to do it' books that came out of the US High Schools' Industrial Arts programs. It does not appear in either the *National Union Catalog*, or in the New York Public Library *Guide to Research Libraries*.

146   VIEWEG, Theodor: *Schiffs-modell-bau im Theorie und Praxis*: 1963.

We have not seen this.

147   VINES, James Cooper: *The Australian Boy's Book of Boats and Model Sailing Yachts*: London and Melbourne, Angus & Robertson, 1934: vi, 71, 4°.

On the title page, the author's name appears as James COOPER-VINES, though in his other books and his magazine writing, he is plain VINES.

Vines was an Australian, though he came to the UK shortly after this book was published. In the late 1930s he was a successful competitor in power straight running competition and was a regular contributor on power boats to *Marine Models*. This is a purely antipodean book, printed in Australia and referring to local suppliers and products, many of which appear to have no UK equivalents.

It is a curious work, of uncertain tone. In some parts it offers abstruse theoretical discussion, in which he assumes his readers will all be familiar with the concept of the parallelogram of forces. He suggests that a few minutes with paper and pencil will enable any boy to work out the appropriate rig for any hull he happens to have. He points his readers towards the scientific study of sail aerodynamics contained in the works of Manfred Curry. Elsewhere, there is some patronising writing down to a juvenile audience.

In his discussion of tools and materials, most of which is entirely standard, he mentions 'Prestwood', an artificial timber made of compressed shavings and available in ⅛ inch and ¼ inch sheets up to eight feet long. It is claimed to be strong, waterproof and uniform in texture, free from any tendency to warp or buckle. It contained no glues or adhesives, cohering only by the effect of pressure on the lignins in the wood. This was presumably an Australian product, as we have seen no reference to it in works published in Europe.

For sails, he suggests 'Japara cloth' as ideal, with linen or unbleached calico as alternatives. What this preferred material can have been is now hard to determine. He claims that Union Silk, the material of choice in the UK, is not known in Australia, which we find hard to credit, given its widespread use by smaller full size racing craft.

For waterproofing, he sets great store by 'Elaterite', a 'mineral rubber'. He claims that, though black and tar like, and never drying out completely, it could be painted over satisfactorily. He mentions a 36 inch power boat hull made of cardboard which he waterproofed with 'Elaterite' to make a very light, 'horn-like', and totally waterproof construction.

The construction methods discussed are carving from the solid, bread and butter and a number of different forms of plank-on-frame construction, all rather sketchy and, as there is no clear indication of the size of boat intended, rather hard to follow. There is one undimensioned plan, that could be for a (not entirely up to date) 10-rater. He also discusses briefly the construction of a sharpie.

Though he mentions the need for mast slides and adjustable mast steps, and treats briefly the use of the Braine gear, he is not really in tune with what serious model yachtsmen were about.

148   WAKELING, Arthur: *Things to Make in Your Home Workshop*: **New York, Grosset and Dunlap, 1939.**
We have not seen this title, but it contains, no doubt among much other material, coverage of what is described as 'The 42 inch National Sea Scout Model'. This may be related to a 42 inch One Design model by Robert Eastburn, originating in the Philadelphia

MYC, published in the British journal *The Model Yachtsman* in 1932.

149   **WALLACE, Carlton (ed):** *The Boy's Book of Hobbies*: **London, Evans Brothers, 1951: 320, 4º.**

The chapter on model ships covers all forms of marine modelling and can only find 7 pages to cover sailing models. There are no plans and no discussion of design. The text is messily organised and far too sketchy to carry a reader through the construction process. Space is wasted in discussing full size techniques such as caulking, before telling the reader that modellers don't do it this way.

The whole thing is wildly out of touch with the realities of supply for model building. Sails may be made from old handkerchiefs 'or get some model yacht cloth from your dealer'. The need to build flow into the sails is recognised, but the writer has wholly inappropriate ideas about how this is to be done. The rigs offered are an over complex bermuda cutter and a very old-fashioned looking gaff sloop. Automatic steering is offered in the form of an eccentric form of reverse tiller gear. This is a very unsatisfactory treatment.

Typically, the one photo illustration is of something far more sophisticated than the writer is capable of. It shows an unidentified 'A' boat 'that won the Challenge Cup in 1949'; but the boat is not *Ranger* that won the *Yachting Monthly* Cup in that year, and the location, that we have not been able to identify, is not Fleetwood. It remains unclear which boat this is and what she won.

*150   **WALTON, James E:** *Model Yachts and Model Yacht Sailing*: **London, Griffith & Farrar, 1879: 104, 8º.**
2nd edition, (though not so described):
London, John Bateman, 1896 : 104, 8º.

Walton, who was a member of the Victoria MYC in East London, shares with Biddle the distinction of being one of the earliest authors of a book on model yachting. Unlike Biddle's, this work is devoted solely to models. It is a slighter work than its competitor and in many ways less sophisticated in its approach and design concepts. It is, for instance, innocent of anything approaching a lines plan, though it does have a fine engraving of a measured drawing of a mackerel. There is also reference to taking 'a plaster cast of the nether portions of a duck' as an inspiration for hull design.

The naivety of the design approach and the crude approach to construction are however linked to a detailed and convincing description of ways to make fittings, rigs and sails. The discussion of sailing technique makes it clear that Walton had extensive practical experience to draw on.

He also describes an extended series of 'scientific' trials of pairs of boats over long open sea courses in an attempt to determine the most effective hull and rig designs. Among other things, these showed conclusively the superiority of loose footed over laced sails, an insight that went largely unregarded for the next seventy years.

The first edition is extremely rare. The second, which is identical, was published by Bateman, who was an engineering and architectural modeller. It is hard to see why he wanted to re-publish Walton when he did; not only is it at variance with his own approach to model making, it was also well out of date by 1896.

A curiosity, both to bibliophiles and to model yachtsmen. A joy to own.

151   WARRING, Ronald Horace: 'Model Yachts', in Staton ABBEY (pseud. William Norman STATON-BEVAN) (Ed): *The Boy's Book of Model Making*: **London and Melbourne, Ward Lock, 1952: 222, 4º.**
This is a chapter in a general compendium of modelling material. Warring, who was primarily an aeromodeller, is operating outside his normal range, which may explain some curiosities if approach. Nonetheless, it is a competent, if brief treatment of hull construction. The sailmaking instructions are minimal and unhelpful; 'seek advice from your local model shop'. There are plans for a boat to the Model Yachting Association's 30 inch Restricted Class, which ignore the abandonment of the class before 1939 after it had failed to attract support. The construction proposed is bread and butter, but in balsa wood, very much an aeromodeller's approach. The sailing instruction includes the use of the Braine gear.

152   WARRING, Ronald Horace: 'Model Yachts':, in Staton ABBEY (pseud. William Norman STATON-BEVAN) (Ed): *Making Model Ships*: **London, Ward Lock, 1957: 80, 4º.**
This repeats identically the material in the preceding entry. The surrounding material is, of course, different. In both books there are photo illustrations of 'A' boats racing at Gosport; one shows 'a Portuguese boat', so must be de Freitas with *Lusitania*, probably in 1948, his first trip to the UK. The other shows a pair starting at Gosport. One is No 510, *Spero*, a Birkenhead boat by J Matchett, that was first registered in 1939 and does not appear to have been

re-registered after the war. There is no record of her participation in the 'A' boat Championships in any year when her registration would have been valid (i.e. 1939, 1948, 1949) and it is not clear when the photo was taken, but presumably after the war.

*153   WEALL, Nick: *Sailing to Win! A Complete Introduction to Model Yacht Racing*: Hemel Hempstead, Argus, 1991: ISBN: 1 85486 077 1: 144, 25 cm.

This is an extremely comprehensive treatment of how to race your boat in modern radio controlled competition, that grew out of a long series of articles in *Model Boats*. Nick is an RYA qualified race judge and, apart from some treatment of sail trim, there is nothing about the boat itself. All is tactics, reading the race and the impact on the tactical situation of the racing Rules. Now somewhat overtaken by changes in the detail of the Rules.

*154   WELLS, Bob: *The Manual for the East Coast 12-Meter*: Mercer Island, WA, Ragged Symmetry, 1995: 214, 27 cm.

This is a detailed handbook, self published by the author, for owners of this one design class, widely sailed in the USA and Australia. There is a brief history of the class and its Rule, and the (not entirely successful) attempts to make it truly a one design class. There are also details of suppliers, construction and finishing techniques. Most of the space is given over to detailed and copiously illustrated instruction on the construction and setting up of the boat, with detailed description of two well known and extremely competitive boats. Finally, some treatment of tuning techniques and radio racing techniques.

Bob writes that he was inspired to put into permanent form the vast amount of lore on the preparation and operation of high class racing boats that had been developed on the EC 12 circuit in the Pacific Northwest. Previously, this had been largely held in the heads of the more experienced skippers and transmitted, if at all, by word of mouth. This admirable aim is extended in later publications from Ragged Symmetry, (Nos. 126, 127)

***155   WILCOCK, A: *Vane Steering Gears*: Watford, Model and Allied Press, 1966, 26, 4º.
Reprinted, 1973.**

Reprinted, Hemel Hempstead, Argus, 1977; 24, 4º.

Wilcock was a member of the Danson club in SE London, and an active skipper and designer of the 1950s and 60s. This text is extracted from a wider ranging series of articles that appeared initially in **Model Maker** in the 1960s. It gives a brief history of the steering devices that preceded the vane gear and a detailed description of the four types of vane then in common use, with a clear assessment of their relative strengths and weaknesses. Most of the text is given over to discussion of the use of the vane in competition.

156   **WILLIAMS, Guy:** *The World of Model Ships and Boats*: **London, Deutsch, New York, G P Putnam's Sons, 1971: 255, 26 cm.**

A large, well illustrated coffee table style of book, covering all forms of marine modelling, but without giving any very solid information on any aspect.

157   **WOOD, John George:** *The Modern Playmate. A Book of Sports. Games and Diversions for Boys of All Ages*: **London, Frederick Warne, n. d., but 1870: x, 883, 8°.**

'New (Revised)' edition: 1875: x, 883, 8°.

As *The Boy's Modern Playmate*; **'New Revised' edition: 1880: x, 883, 8°.**

'Revised' edition, 1890: x, 816, 8°.

'New Edition, Thoroughly Revised': 1906: x, 816, 8°.

This is a huge compendium of indoor and outdoor games and amusements and is clearly the work of many hands. The 1870 edition may not be the first, as the British Library copies are all late acquisitions. The discussion of the Rules of Football shows that this part of the text at least was written after the 1863 Cambridge meeting that established the FA. There is some discussion of full size sailing, but the model sailing is included under 'Shipbuilding' in the section on 'The Young Workman'.

This includes rather basic instruction for carving a hull from the solid and for a conventional plank-on-frame hull, though this uses a crude method that dispenses with a building board.

There is also a very curious idea for a planked hull that is built by first carving from a block, then slicing the hull up horizontally and reducing the lifts from inside to plank thickness, finally re-assembling the pieces and reinforcing the structure with internal metal ribs cut from copper.

The directions are both confused and confusing and seem uncertain whether the aim is to replicate full size practice or produce something more practical as a model. There is no instruction on how to sail the model. This is probably just as well as the whole approach is so casual ('the false keel, which may as well be of lead...') that it is unlikely that any boats were built from these suggestions. By contrast, the adjacent section on 'The Amateur Engineer' is fuller, more competent and more practical.

158   **YATES Raymond Francis:** *The Boy's Book of Model Boats*: **New York, The Century Publishing Co., 1920: viii, 215, 8°.**
2nd (Revised) edition: New York and London, Appleton-Century, 1943: xi, 274, 8°.

The author claims to have been an ardent boat enthusiast as a boy and to have scoured the shelves of his local library without success for a book that would 'tell him something about boats, and especially information about the construction of models', vowed that on becoming a man, he would write such a book.

In all fairness he tried but failed lamentably, mainly because he attempted too much. Clearly aimed at children, it is both simplistic and sketchy, veering between the ridiculously crude and the unreasonably complex. It is not easy to describe the construction of a flash steam plant in language that is meaningful to the average 12 year old, let alone expect him to follow such instructions.

It is not until page 164 that Yates reaches sailing models. His one virtue is that he there reproduces, with due acknowledgement, not only the plans for a 24 inch model by W J Daniels that appeared in *Junior Mechanics* in 1914, but the complete text of the article and the accompanying detail drawings.

The second edition reproduces the contents of the first and adds chapters on petrol-engined hydroplanes, which had clearly become Yates' own main interest. He was a member of a club that raced them on Conservatory Pond in Central Park and donated trophies for their competitions. The yachting material remains encapsulated in the high class amber of WJD's 1914 practice.

This is a much less convincing work than his *Model Making* of 1919, (No. 198) which is described in the section on the history of radio control. He clearly knew what he was about, so his failure here must be attributed to his misjudgement of what was required for a juvenile audience.

*159   ZWALGUN, Emil: *Modellsegeln; Theorie und*
Trimm, mit Klassen- und Wettsegelbestimmungen
des DSV Modellsegelabteilung: Berlin, Delius,
Klasing & Co. 1941.

We have not seen this; it appears to be only a brief text and, from
the description in an advertisement included in **de BRUYCKER**
(No. 17) deals with sailing techniques and includes the DSV rating
and racing Rules, as well as instructions for the building of a model
yacht lake. Zwalgun was an experienced modeller and skippered
Emmy, the German challenger for the *Yachting Monthly* Cup in
1929. Like Tiller and other German writers, he published a number
of model yacht designs during and after the war years.

THE DEVELOPMENT OF RADIO CONTROL

The importance of radio control to the development of model yachting in the last thirty years or so is such that it is worth recording at least some of the development of control systems. This section does not pretend to be a complete bibliography of this complex subject; in particular, we have made no systematic study of the large periodical literature for wireless amateurs, which carried much of the story of radio control development, in the period when it was still a black art.

Before the mid-1970s there is no book that contains any significant amount of information on the radio control of sailing models. The few that do offer this sort of coverage come late in time and have been included in the main model yachting section of this bibliography.

In this section, we comment in detail on some of the many books that have tackled the subject from a broader perspective, but the genre may readily be divided into two groups, by their date and by the nature of their content.

The earlier, 'phase one', group are largely concerned, many of them wholly concerned, with the design and construction of radio systems and are written by radio experimenters. Only when radio had ceased to require both a knowledge of electronic theory and skill in winding coils and the use of a soldering iron, is there much treatment of the **use** of radio in models. One gets the impression that relatively few of the wireless experimenters ever ventured their creations in the air or on the water. Certainly they were content to show that their systems worked, rather than to use radio to develop new styles of activity and sporting competition.

After about 1960, 'phase two' texts begin to be written; theory, circuit diagrams and instructions on the tuning of systems start to disappear and to be replaced by installation instructions and diagrams of aerobatic patterns and other descriptions of things to do with a radio controlled model. This marks the beginning of the transition from radio control as a toy for wireless experts to radio as a tool for modellers, which would ultimately transform the nature of model sports.

The first British magazine devoted entirely to radio controlled models (and from its inception, almost exclusively to aircraft models), *Radio Control Models and Electronics*, dates from 1960.

By 1970, there is a plethora of books introducing the beginner to radio control, usually in the context of model aircraft. Hardly any of these give much information on how a radio system works, let alone how to build one, but all give lots of space to installation and operation. Repair is treated in terms of 'keep a note of the service agent's address'

Warring's book (No. 195) is the only one explicitly to recognise the very different nature of these two enterprises and to express an opinion on the practicality of the devices developed by the earlier radio experimenters.

It must be recognised that the radio control of sailing models is very much a peripheral and minority interest within the radio modelling arena. The vast bulk of equipment is developed for and sold to aeromodellers. The American *Radio Control Buyer's Guide,*[9] a compendium of commercially available equipment and models, makes this clear. The 3rd edition of 1977 contains 50 pages of kits for aircraft models, 4 of competition power boat kits, 3 of scale and sport power models and 2 of sailing craft. Of the 8 sail kits offered, all but one are for boats designed to one or other of the AMYA's recognised racing classes.

The 11th edition of 1987 has 67 pages of aircraft, 12 of power boats of all descriptions and a page and a half of sailing craft. By this date, only one of the 9 kits offered is for an AMYA class. The suppliers recognised that the specialist demands and rapid design revision called for in the small market for serious competition vehicles could not easily be combined with the long production runs needed in the commercial world.

One result of the peripheral position of sailing craft in the radio controlled modelling spectrum is that the provision of sail winches, (the only special to function element in a model yacht), has remained very largely in the hands of specialist 'cottage industry' suppliers, drawn from the model yachting community. This is especially the case with winches offering very low weight or other features particularly desirable to the competitive skipper.

---

[9] 3rd edition, Clifton, VA, Boynton Associates, 1977: 208, 4°:
    11th edition, Clifton, VA, Boynton Associates, 1987: 352, 4°:

BOOKS ON RADIO CONTROL

160   **ALDRIDGE, D W:** *Transistorised Radio Control of Models*: **London, Foulsham, 1973**

This is not in the British Library, though it appears from the *Cumulative Book Index* to be a UK originated title. Many of Foulsham's other technical manuals were imports from the USA. We have not seen it, but assume it is a relatively late example of the radio expert's approach to radio control. It is the only title we know of that appears to take explicit account of the transistor revolution and its effect on the design of radio gear.

161   **BOWMAN, Mogen:** *Radiostyring af Modelskibe*: **Stockholm, Teknisk Verlag, 1974.**

We have not seen this.

162   **CAMM, Frederick James:** *Radio Controlled Models*: **London, Pearson, 1958: 184, 8º.**
Second edition, with additional material by A T COLLINS, London, Pearson, 1963: 192, 8º.

This was one of the last of Camm's many books, and drew on articles he had written in *Practical Mechanics*, of which he was editor, and other material that had appeared in the newsletter of the International Radio Controlled Model Society. In the introduction Camm recalls that he has been both an aeromodeller and a radio experimenter over many years, but regards the development of radio control of models as a post war phenomenon. This is slightly at variance with our own perception of the strict truth, but undoubtedly true as regards the existence of a critical mass of hobbyists interested in the problems.

He attributes post war development of a radio control constituency to three factors:

> the experience which the war gave to many servicemen of operating radio equipment, and thus a grounding in the technology and underlying theory;

> the availability of miniature compression ignition 'diesel' engines which were cheaper and easier to manage than the petrol fuelled, spark ignition, engines that had been the norm before 1939;

> the availability of a wide range of compact (and cheap) components on the war surplus market.

This combination of factors, he argues, sparked a boom in experimentation in the radio control of models, mainly in the context of aircraft and power boats.

The organisation of the book is interesting. It starts with a description of the most essential part of the inter-gear, a rudder operating mechanism. Only then does he describe simple single valve receiver circuits and associated transmitters. There is also material on mechanically generated mark/space signals for proportional control, the use of mark/space to produce a second channel and on more sophisticated six-valve systems, allowing sufficient discrimination to operate two models simultaneously. His description of such a system remarks that tuning is sensitive to temperature, and thus the boat should be placed in the water for ten to fifteen minutes with the radio on before final tuning of the receiver is attempted.

His more sophisticated systems also include reed based receivers, which he rather confusingly describes as 'audio control', and a complete chapter on the design and tuning of transmitter aerials to ensure maximum radiation efficiency. There is also a chapter on the construction of essential test equipment. These include yet another version of the bulb based field strength meter and an automatic transmitter switching device to facilitate the essential range checks when operating single handed.

The second edition, which appeared after Camm's death, contains an additional chapter by Collins, who replaced him as editor of *Practical Mechanics*. This returns to the problem of aerial efficiency and advocates the use of a tuner to ensure that the output is in the most efficient form to suit the relationship between the length of the aerial and the transmission wavelength.

163   CONNOLLY, Philip and SMEED, Victor Ernest:
         Radio Control for Model Boats: Hemel Hempstead,
         MAP, 1970: 128, 21cm.

This is a 'second phase' book. There is very little about radio control and a lot about how to install the gear in a boat, together with material on the design of suitable hulls for power boat competition, the care and maintenance of power plants and the like. There is no material specifically on sailing craft installation.

There is discussion of different types of commercial servos, many of which still closely resemble the home built devices of an earlier era. A final chapter discusses the transistor and transistor circuits as recent and much more reliable switching devices than relays.

164   CUNDELL, John: *Radio Control in Model Boats*:
Hemel Hempstead, Argus, 1989: ISBN 1 854 8602 X:
174, 21 cm.

This is an update of the previous entry, written by the present editor of *Model Boats*. It covers much the same ground as its predecessor, but reflects the current state of the commercial supply of radio gear. It now includes a chapter on installations in sailing craft.

165   HILDEBRAND, Ludwig: *Electronische
Fernegesteuring*: Berlin, Schneider, 1952: 64,
22cm.
2nd Edition: Berlin, Schneider, 1957.

We have not seen this relatively early German treatment of radio control techniques.

166   HONNEST REDLICH, George: *Radio Control for
Models*: Leighton Buzzard, Harborough, 1950: 128,
8º.

This is a comprehensive coverage of the state of the art at the time of its publication. It even includes a brief historical introduction that credits Branly with the first demonstration of action at a distance in Paris in 1905 and emphasises the slow and difficult progress until the US development of the thyratron valve specifically for radio control applications in the late 1930s. He implies that these valves had only become available in the UK in very recent years.

He writes that the tuned reed was developed in parallel in the US, in France and in Britain. He claims that R/C is now (1950) on the point of becoming available to all, rather than to a closed circle of experts, as its methods are becoming sufficiently standardised to give a satisfactory degree of reliability.

What this really means is that his employers were offering commercially produced complete systems, which they wished to sell more widely. The true popularisation of radio control would take another ten years at least. More importantly, as he himself acknowledges, progressive, rather than simple 'bang-bang' control, needed for serious acrobatic flying and for control of yacht sheeting, called for more complex circuits, which at that date implied seriously decreased reliability.

His discussion of intergear ranges far and wide, from simple rubber driven actuators, through servo motors with solenoid operated 'drop in' worm drives, (an exactly similar system to that used by **Pettman** in 1911). (See No.177) He also discusses a mark/space system derived directly from the *Knüppel* control used in German glider bombs in WW II, but his main pitch is for the tuned reed.

His discussion of the control of sailing yachts assumes that only the rudder will be controlled, and that this will influence the design of the boat to optimise performance under this constraint. Within a few months of publication however, he was demonstrating an 'A' boat with both rudder and sail control, though with only a three-position sheet adjustment.

167   **HUNDLEBY, H G:** *Simple Radio Control*: **Watford, Model Aeronautical Press, 1955: 96, 8⁰. eight reprints to 1959.**

2nd Edition, Revised by Thomas H IVES: Watford, MAP, 1961: 96, 8⁰.

Both editions are clearly 'phase one' texts, and are important because they were published by the leading model publishing house, rather than by a radio specialists' outlet. The number of reprints of the first edition suggests that a very high proportion of the sets built in the 1950s must have drawn heavily on this source.

Hundleby envisages construction from scratch, with detailed instruction on soldering technique and emphasis on the importance of careful construction of the meter. The main transmitter and receiver designs are the *Aeromodeller* designs, first described there by Howard Boys in 1951 and 52, though not designed by him. Great emphasis is laid on the need to follow the design precisely and to avoid the temptation to 'improve' it. Actuators are the only element not to be wholly home built and Hundleby suggests a range of commercial products, two of which are only available as military surplus items.

The second edition is much the same in style, but includes the *Aeromodeller* transistor receiver. This adds a couple of transistors to the standard valve based regenerative set to improve range and reliability and (most important) to reduce the voltage requirement to (only) 22 volts, with useful savings in airborne weight. The author takes the view that a fully transistorised design running on only 9 volts is still beyond the capability of the home constructor. There is some treatment in this edition of ways of getting proportional control from a single channel set, by means of a 'galloping ghost' mechanism driven by a mechanical mark/space generator.

The aircraft designs offered are unchanged in the second edition, but much can be learned by comparing the advertisements in the two editions, which show a very substantial development in the availability of commercially produced radio gear and a wide range of aircraft kits designed for use with radio. There is no specific treatment of models other than aircraft.

168　　　HUNT, Peter: *Radio Control for Model Aircraft*:
　　　Leicester, Harborough, 1942: 64, 8°.

A very early account of what was clearly a practical working radio system, installed in a very large model aircraft, (the wingspan must have been over eight feet and twin petrol engines were used). The vehicle needed to be large, as Hunt enthusiastically claims that the weight of the airborne installation could with care be reduced to about six pounds. The emphasis throughout is on a simple and practical approach, relying on a powerful transmitter signal to overcome the low efficiency of the receiver circuits used, and the difficulty of tuning the system accurately to suit flight conditions.

Discussing the possibility of electric motors to power servo mechanisms, Hunt remarks that they are admirable, but it is impossible to find them small and light enough for the purpose, and equally difficult to make something suitable from scratch.

A minor problem is to decide where, when and how Hunt conducted his flight trials. Private radio transmissions of all kinds were prohibited during the war, but all the illustrations of the author building and flying his model show him in the uniform of an RAF Flight Lt., with pilot's wings. During the war he must surely have had more important things to do than play with toy planes. Presumably, the experiments reported date from before September 1939.

169　　　JOHNSON, Valentine Edward: *Modern Models*:
　　　London, Pearson ('How Does it Work' Series),
　　　1914: 126, 8°.
　　　Also in an edition in a common binding with
　　　another of the 'How Does it Work' series
　　　Submarine Engineering **by S F WALKER.**
　　　London, Pearson, 1914: 128 and 126, 8°.

Johnson was a mathematician who wrote widely on popular science topics from the late 1880s. He was a founder member of the Royal Aeronautical Society and 'models editor' of the magazine *Flight* in the years before 1914; his later work has a strong aeronautical component.

The treatment of actual construction of the model aircraft, (including 'hydro-aeroplanes'), submarines and boats is sketchy, but the book is important as (probably) the first popular treatment of the possibilities of radio control. In its coverage of electrical and mechanical devices and experiments, it deals with an adaptation of a Wimshurst machine to generate wireless waves, by which the experimenter is able to control action at a distance.

In this case, nothing more exciting is attempted than switching lights on the other side of the room, as is the case in his parallel *Electrical Recreations* (London, Marshall, n.d., but 1920s), where such activity is envisaged as part of an electrical entertainment or conjuring show.

170   **JOHNSON, Valentine Edward:** *The Theory and Practice of Model Aeroplaning*: **London, E & F N Spon, 1910; New York, Spon and Chamberlain, 1910: xv, 148, 8⁰.**
2nd edition. London, Spon, 1920: vii, 257, 8⁰.
reprinted, 1930.

The first edition of this standard work is wholly concerned with the model flying scene before 1914.

In chapter VIII of the second, expanded, edition, Johnson discusses the development of radio control technology since he first wrote, and draws attention to the relevant patents from the period immediately before 1914, together with pre-war and wartime work on radio controlled weapons. He urges modellers and wireless experimenters to co-operate in developing viable wireless systems for the control of models. It is however fairly clear that he has no actual experience of attempting the task himself. He makes no direct reference to the work of those like **Pettman** and **Phillips**, who were already experimenting in this field.

171   **JUDD, F C:** *Radio Control for Model Ships, Boats and Aircraft*: **London, Data Publications, 1954: vi, 140, 8⁰.**
2nd edition, 1962, 192, 8⁰.
reprinted, 1968.

This text originally appeared as articles in various magazines from 1951 onwards. A radio enthusiast's approach, full of theory, circuit diagrams and test instruments. Next to nothing on how to use the systems in models.

The second edition is considerably different, with much less theory and radio data. There is an extended section on servo mechanisms and controls by **Raymond F STOCK**, which is extremely comprehensive.

172   KEARNEY, Jean Michel: *Radio Controlled Models for Amateurs*: London, Bernard (Bernard's Series, No. 133), 1955: vi, 74, 4º.

This is one of a wide range of technical manuals on radio and television published by Bernard's. It claims in its introduction to be, 'though not the first book on radio control, the first to give ALL the information required in a clear form.'

It is very ambitious in its approach, and advanced for its date. The relatively short text builds up from the simplest forms of single channel gear to multi-channel proportional systems with crystal control of frequency. Kearney is dismissive of simple forms of control and emphasises that they can only give 'bang-bang' control. 'Proper' radio control needs both multiple channels and proportional movement. The first can be achieved by audio tone modulation with discrimination in the receiver either by tuned reeds or by tuned chokes.

Proportional control can be achieved from single channel gear by use of a mark/ space system, or by electronic modulation of tone for 'true' proportional operation. These are the underlying techniques of all later systems and were clearly understood by radio experimenters even at this early date. This is perhaps not so surprising; what is striking is that Kearney clearly believes that the home construction of such systems is within the capacity of the average amateur radio constructor.

Though he writes with authority about the inter gear needed to apply radio control to aircraft, it is clear that Kearney is much more interested in the radio than the model.

173   MIESSNER, Benjamin Franklin: *Radiodynamics*: New York, Van Nostrand; London, Lockwood, 1916: 206, 8º.

174   MIESSNER, Benjamin Franklin: *On the Early History of Radio Guidance*: San Francisco, San Francisco Press, 1964: vi, 64, 8º.

Meissner was an early radio engineer. The son of a mid-western store owner, he could not afford to go to college and joined the US Navy as an enlisted man. He worked in the radio station of the Washington Navy Yard, when this was also the main Radio R&D facility for the service. As he tells it, he and his enlisted colleagues from the Navy Yard went on to become the founders of the radio industry in America. After leaving the service he worked (1911-12) as the sole technical assistant to John Hays Hammond, a wealthy and (according to Meissner) dilettante experimenter who was working on radio controlled torpedo projects.

Radiodynamics is his contemporary, serious, engineer's account of the state of play in radio control in the immediate pre-war years. There is a sound, if brief, survey of predecessors from Tesla in the 1890s and a detailed account of the experiments he had been involved in. The radio circuits he uses are much more up to date than those used by Phillips (No 177), being based on de Forest's recently developed thermionic valve. There are also brief treatments of the possibility of acoustic homing torpedoes and a description of a 'bug' that would follow a line on the lab floor by means of light sensitive receptors.

In old age, he wrote the story again, partly as a memoir, partly as a contribution to an ongoing debate among radio engineers over the priority that may or may not have been due to Hammond for the development of effective radio control. It gives a much more personalised account, claiming for himself, with evidence from his research notebooks of the period, many advances for which Hammond had sought credit.

175   MODEL BOATS: *Model Boats Radio Control Handbook*: **Hemel Hempstead, Model and Allied Publications, 1968: 36, 12°.**
A very simple guide to the possibilities of radio control in model boats of all types. The main emphasis is on powered models, but there is a section on the application of radio to sailing models.

The emphasis is on the essential tuning and adjustment of the still primitive radio gear of the period. Many advertisements from suppliers give a good picture of the state of the market as radio passed from being a black art to a relatively cheap and reliable technology available to non-specialist users.

176   PACKARD, Robert Henry: 'An Improved Radio-Controlled Sailboat', in *Radio-craft*, **November 1935, 266ff.**
This is the leading item in a pack of press cuttings, copies of which we were given by the developer when we met him sixty years after he had built his experimental radio controlled model. They describe a radio controlled 48 inch ketch built by a young Harvard graduate over the previous few years. As well as this technical description, there are reports of the boat in the *Boston Globe* and *Boston Traveler* in October 1934 and his home town paper, the Salem *News,* for 27 September 1933.

Control is to both rudder and sails and is probably the first such installation to be described. The gear, which was all built from scratch, uses a single valve receiver to drive a selector with silver contacts inset into a bakelite disc. The single motor is used for both rudder and sail control, by means of what the Boston Globe describes as 'a simple gear shifting arrangement'.

177   PETTMAN, J S: 'Model Power Boat Control by Wireless', in *Model Engineer*, 23, (1910), 57-61.

This is the earliest description we have found of a practical radio control system for a model boat. The model is an electrically powered semi scale destroyer with a hull 62 inches by 7 by 6. The displacement is 28 pounds and the speed is said to be five knots. It is, as the author himself admits, entirely unremarkable.

The radio system is the standard spark generator and coherer of the period. The on-board equipment includes a coherer, a relay, a large number of magnetic switches and solenoids, four driving motors, a steering motor and a set of 6 volt, 30 amp/hour accumulators for the radio. The propulsion motors are driven by a separate 12 volt supply.

The guts of the control system is a sequential switcher, which uses ten separate 'events' to give five functions, i.e. left rudder, right rudder, motor on forward, motor off, motor on reverse. The steering motor drives the rudder through a worm and wheel. The worm is engaged on the wheel by means of a substantial solenoid, and is in contact only while the motor is driving it. Only a segment of the wheel retains its teeth so that the rudder can be held at a 30 degree deflection. When the current is off, the solenoid releases the worm from the wheel which is self centring by means of a spring.

As the steering motor and the four propulsion motors are all shunt wound, reversing them is a major operation. The 12v propulsion motors need a separate and substantial switch system. Pettman dreamed up a rocking arm switch that dipped carbon rods into mercury filled cups. It looks like nothing so much as a walking beam engine, as used on Hudson river steam boats. Pettman comments 'a more unsuitable material cannot possibly be imagined than mercury, where employed in a portable form, unless special precautions are employed. I would suggest that carbon blocks are substituted for the mercury cups.'

The impression is of a system thought out from first principles, with some ingenious solutions to the problems of transforming radio signals into control actions. Many of these problems arise from the decision to use shunt wound motors rather than permanent magnet types. Possibly at this date, permanent magnet motors of sufficient power were not available. **Phillips** also used shunt wound motors in his closely contemporary airship project.

The whole thing seems, to modern eyes, massively over engineered and constructed without any thought for weight control. All the same, there is every indication that it worked.

178   PHILLIPS, Raymond: *Radio Controlled Mechanisms for Amateurs*: London, Cassell, (Amateur Wireless Handbooks), 1927: 111, 8°.

Phillips was a radio experimenter who, as early as 1911, had demonstrated a radio controlled airship from the stage of the London Hippodrome. His patent for the system he used (Class 40, Wireless Signalling, etc. 6316) is dated 10 March 1910.

In this 1927 handbook he describes in detail the radio system and inter-gear that he used for this machine. It is based on the original wireless technology of spark gap transmitter and coherer based receiver, which Phillips still prefers to valve based circuits for control applications. The rest of the book is taken up with discussion of the possibility of applying wireless control to other forms of model, including railways and boats. The system he proposes for boats, using a solenoid control for the rudder, required considerable currents and thus substantial battery capacity and would only have been suitable for relatively large models. He himself dismisses the possibility of controlling either sails or steam plant, but thinks that an electrically powered boat might be controlled satisfactorily. It is not clear whether he had actually tried his boat control ideas.

We can find no reference to Phillips' pre-1914 work in *Model Engineer,* and he makes no mention of some rather different, and in some ways more practical, approaches to boat control that were reported there before the war. It may be that he regarded himself primarily as a stage entertainer, since his book also contains ideas for 'mind reading' acts and other stage illusions making use of radio.

179   PHILLIPS, Raymond: *Ray Controlled Mechanisms*: London, Percival Marshall (Model Engineer Handbooks), 1933: 96, 8°.

This is very much a repeat of Phillips' earlier title with some additional matter, most of it speculative and theoretical, on rays other than radio as the basis for control of mechanisms at a distance. There is brief treatment of sound, light and infra-red control possibilities.

180   RAYER, F G: *Radio Control for Beginners*:
London, Bernard Babani, 1980: iv, 92, 8⁰.

A very late example of a 'phase one' book, written wholly for radio enthusiasts and envisaging an entirely home built system. There is no discussion of transistor circuits and even the mark-space device proposed is electro-mechanical in operation.

181   ROCKWOOD, E L: *Audio Tone Control*: **USA, 1949.**

We have not seen this title, which is described by other writers of the period as the leading authority on the development of tuned reed control. There is no record of it in any of the US bibliographical sources we have used; possibly it is not a book but a series of articles in a periodical.

182   SAFFORD, Edward Lenfesty, Jr.: *Model Radio Control*: **New York, Gernsback, 1959: 192, 8⁰.**

Safford's extensive writings on radio control are a good example of the progress of one man from the radio experimenter's approach to radio control to that of the very expert and demanding user.

Safford however, was no amateur tinkerer. One of his books describes him as 'Training Supervisor in the Missile Sciences Division of the Electronics Department at Fort Bliss'. This was, and is, the US Army's main research and development establishment for missiles, so Safford was clearly a professional in his field and in his working life operating at the cutting edge of the available control technology, without too much financial restraint. Some of this can be seen in the content and general approach of his books for modellers. We have not been able to trace anything he may have written on control technology in the military context.

This earliest volume is presented as 'a complete revision' of a title that originally appeared in 1951. We have not seen the earlier version, but this is one of a wide range of technical radio handbooks published by Gernsback. It gives a comprehensive treatment from first principles of how R/C works, with extensive guidance on the building and tuning of radio gear.

This title deals only with single channel super-regenerative systems and assumes that any one who can solder can build effective equipment for themselves. He does, however, give coverage of the gear that was then commercially available in the USA, especially when he moves on to discuss the decoding elements of the system. As in most radio manuals of this period, the decoding and inter-gear options are the element most fully discussed and a very wide variety of possible systems are treated. There is some discussion of tuned reed decoders, but he does not favour them. The discussion of transistors is extremely brief and though their potential advantage over valves is acknowledged, they are not employed in the circuits that are offered.

Though a little later in date than the second edition of **Sommerhoff** (No.191), this is not as advanced in its concepts and may not be as much revised from the 1951 edition as the publisher would wish us to believe.

183   SAFFORD, Edward Lenfesty, Jr.: *The Radio
             Control Manual*: New York, Gernsback, 1961: 192,
             8⁰.

Where the preceding item of 1959 (or 1951) is all about pulse coders and decoders, this is even more basic in its approach and assumes nothing of its readers. 'The first test, soldering'.

Safford clearly envisages a totally home built system, including the servos, and discusses both two channel systems using tone filter decoding and 'galloping ghost' systems as a means of achieving pulsed proportional control. To produce more than two channels, he describes a split in US practice between West coat modellers, who favoured tone decoders and proportional control, while in the East, the preferred approach was to use reed decoders.

184   SAFFORD, Edward Lenfesty, Jr.: *The Radio
             Control Manual*: Blue Ridge Summit, PA, TAB,
             1968. vi, 192, 8⁰.
             **English edition, with an introduction for
             English readers by W Oliver: Slough,
             Foulsham-TAB, 1973: viii, 192, 8⁰.**

This is a different text from the Gernsback volume of similar title.

Still concerned with the home builder, Safford now offers both valve and transistor based receiver designs, but the illustrations are almost exclusively of commercially available complete systems, mainly of the 'Citizenship' range. The construction of servos from scratch is dealt with, but there is also discussion of kit built and commercial products.

The installation discussion covers aircraft and cars in considerable detail. There is also a brief treatment of sailing models, based on fitting out a Dumas kit for a Marblehead closely based on the full size Star class form, using a Dumas sail control unit. This is based on a jockey travelling on a threaded rod. There is some very basic discussion of sailing technique. There is not room for more as the six pages available are largely taken up with photos showing the radio installation. The treatment of power boat installation is even more cursory.

The English introduction, which also appears in many other Foulsham editions of TAB titles, is a mere three pages and covers only the different radio regulation and licensing requirements in the UK and details of local suppliers.

185   **SAFFORD, Edward Lenfesty, Jr.:** *Advanced Radio Control*: **Blue Ridge Summit, PA, TAB, 1965: iv, 192, 21cm. 8⁰.**
            English edition, Slough, Foulsham-TAB, 1973: vii, 192, 8⁰.

This is just what its title suggests, a treatment of radio design and construction with emphasis on ways of coping with what were perceived as problems and deficiencies in current practice, in particular the design and construction of truly proportional servos.

Reflecting Safford's day job, there are chapters on radio control of rockets, including some discussion of vehicle design and propellant characteristics and a chapter on the design of radio controlled robot figures.

186   **SAFFORD, Edward Lenfesty, Jr:** *The Radio Control Hobbyists Handbook*: **Blue Ridge Summit, PA, TAB, 1984: xii, 340, 8⁰.**

This is all 'phase two'; it assumes the use of commercial equipment and the universality of digital proportional control. Most of the discussion is of the refinements of the basic concept that were becoming available, including the pros and cons of dual rate and non linear servo response, as well as mixing and pre-programming of signals, 'used only by competitive pylon racers'. On the other hand, servo reversal from the transmitter is seen as having universal application. The discussion of means of changing the frequency is primitive by UK standards and suggests that even at this date, interchangeable crystals were a rarity in the US.

The installation section is concerned mainly with aircraft and helicopter models, with sections also on rocketry and robots. There is no discussion of sailing models, possibly because they have little call for the subtleties of radio function that Safford finds so interesting. There is extended treatment of flying technique particularly of advanced manoeuvres.

Unusually, attention is paid to organisational issues, with extended discussion of club organisation and the running of flying sites, paying close attention to safety. Safford argues that the increasing congestion of frequency bands can be tackled both by the government increasing the allocation of frequencies for model use and by improving the discrimination of radio equipment to make better use of the space available.

It looks as though this is the book that Safford wrote after he had retired from government service and was able to devote his considerable expertise exclusively to radio control as a hobby.

187   SCHMIDT, R C and L A WILLIAMS: 'A Radio Controlled Model Sailboat', in *Radio News*, April 1948, 39-42.

This is a brief description, in a US radio experimenters' journal. of an installation by two Boston based radio enthusiasts for the control of an 'A' boat. Only the rudder is controlled and because of the size of the boat it is driven by a permanent magnet motor. To avoid the delay inherent in a selector, the authors choose to employ two entirely separate single-valve super-regenerative receivers, operating on widely spaced frequency bands of 51 and 53 Mhz. Left and right rudder movements were achieved by switching the transmitter from one frequency to another, with a central position in which it was transmitting on neither. The rudder could be run from full left to full right in about 15 seconds.

This is very much a radio experimenter's approach and most of the text is given over to describing the circuits and the procedures for tuning the system.

188   SIPOSS, George: *Model Sail and Power Boating by Remote Control*: Blue Ridge Summit, PA, TAB, 1974: 192, 8o.
Slough, Foulsham-TAB, 1975: 192, 8º.

A 'second phase' book, almost entirely concerned with the installation and use of commercial radio equipment. 'Today, you can get all you need in five minutes at your local hobby store.'

It contains an early treatment of the basics of radio controlled sailing. Rather less than half the text is devoted to sailing craft, with a chapter of rather elementary sail aerodynamic theory, one on the construction of models from glass reinforced plastic kits and a brief treatment of racing organisation and rules.

189   SMEED, Victor Ernest: *Introducing Radio Control Model Boats*: Hemel Hempstead, Argus, 1983: 92, 21cm.

A very general coverage of all forms of radio controlled marine models, which can be rather confusing, as it jumps from topic to topic. A useful introduction, if now a little out of date.

190   SOMMERHOFF, Gerald Walter Christian: *Radio Control of Models*: London, Norman Price, 1954: ix, 70, 8°.

191   SOMMERHOFF, Gerald Walter Christian: *Radio Control of Model Aircraft*: London, Percival Marshall, 1954: iv, 164, 8°. **2nd, revised, edition, 1957: ix, 70, 8°.**

Sommerhoff was a science master at the Dragon School, Oxford and experimented widely with radio control, aided by the members of the school's Science Club. His books are almost entirely concerned with aircraft, but give a good conspectus of what was possible with single channel super-regenerative apparatus.

The first edition of *R/C of Model Aircraft* contains details of his patented mark-space apparatus, by which it was possible to extract two simultaneous controls from a single channel system. This disappears from the much shorter second edition, which carries information, absent from the 1954 text, on the use of transistors, but still not in the primary detector circuits, and more detail of the increasing range of commercial equipment available.

192   WARRING, Ronald Horace: *Radio Controlled Models: Model Aircraft, Boats and Land Vehicles*: London, Museum Press, 1962: 136, 8°.

Warring was an immensely prolific technical author with over 90 titles recorded from the late 1930s onwards, mainly in the field of model aircraft. Here he gives a brief rundown of the technical advances, but this title treats all parts of the system other than escapements and servos as black boxes with which the modeller need not concern himself. In this it is an early example of the 'black box' approach to radio control.

193   WARRING, Ronald Horace: *Scientific Hobbies for Boys*: London, Lutterworth Press, 1963: 172, 8°.

Chapter 12 of this book deals with radio control of models. It discusses home building only to make clear that it is not for the inexperienced. 'There are many pitfalls and the results are usually very disappointing.' Building from kits is cheaper than buying ready made equipment, but much can still go wrong and the costs can still be high. There is a correlation between reliability and expense, and the expense must be accepted, because reliability is paramount, especially for the operation of aircraft.

There is brief discussion of broad types of commercial equipment, all valve based and mainly very simple. Tuned reeds are touched upon as the way to achieve multi-channel control.

Suitable reed systems are said to cost £100 for a transmitter-receiver combo and £10 a time for servos.

194   **WARRING, Ronald Horace:** *Multi-Channel Radio Control*: **Hemel Hempstead, Model and Allied Publications, 1966: 112, 8º.**

This is wholly devoted to the needs of the modeller using commercial equipment 'because the home building of the more sophisticated systems is too demanding'. Nearly all the multi channel systems discussed are based on reed filters.

195   **WARRING, Ronald Horace:** *A Beginner's Guide to Radio Control*: **Guildford and London, Lutterworth Press, 1967: 159, 8º.**
                       2nd edition, 1972: 171, 8º.

This title is notable in that its first chapter is not on 'The Principles of Radio', but on 'The Development of Radio Control' and gives an unvarnished history of the uncertain progress in the field. This draws attention to the impracticality of much of the radio gear designed by radio experts for its nominal purpose of controlling models, and thus to the importance of a very small group in the US who, combining radio knowledge with modelling experience, did most of the work in developing practical, robust and reliable systems.

He dates the initial availability of commercially produced multi-proportional systems to 1963-65, and their more general availability to the entry of Japanese manufacturers into mass production, and thus to significant falls in cost, in the later 1960s. Writing after multi-proportional systems had become generally available, he dismisses out of hand nearly all earlier systems developed to give multi-channel proportional control from a single channel transmission as 'fit to operate only on the test bench.'

196   **WARRING, Ronald Horace:** *Radio Control for Modellers*: **Guildford, Lutterworth Press, 1981: 132, 23cm.**

This is the last of Warring's radio control books and deals only with the installation of commercial equipment. All is multi channel, digital proportional and with crystal controlled frequencies. The opening of the first chapter witnesses to the effects of the transistor revolution and of the commercialisation of radio control production in the previous ten years or so.

> The modern radio control outfit is designed to be as nearly foolproof as possible. It requires no adjustment. No wiring up is required, since

components that have to be connected are pre-wired and fitted with plug and socket connections.

Despite its late date, the book contains no mention of radio in sailing models.

197   WINTER, William: *Radio Control for Model Builders*: New York, Rider; London, Chapman & Hall, 1960: viii, 220, 8º.

A comprehensive American treatment, specifically aimed at the modeller as **user** of radio control and dealing largely with the commercially available systems and how to use them, rather than with how to design and build radio gear. Though new in its orientation, and in its treatment of such new ideas as transistors, hand held transmitters and tuned reed filters for multi-tone transmissions, this book is on the cusp of the transition to 'radio as a black box'. A field strength meter is still regarded as an essential part of every operator's equipment.

198   YATES, Raymond Francis: *Model Making for the Professional and Amateur Mechanic; Instruction on Processes and Operations involved in Model Making and the Actual Construction of Numerous Models, including Steam Engines, etc; Pattern Work, Lathe Work, Electroplating, Soft and Hard Soldering, Grinding and Drilling are also Included*: New York, Norman W Henly Publishing, London, Hodder & Stoughton, 1919: 390, 8º. Reprint, New York, Lindsay, 1985.

In marked contrast to his model boat title for boys, (No. 158) this is a very serious, very advanced, and very competent manual of model engineering addressed to adults. Yates is described as editor of *Everyday Engineering* and it is clear from his record of publications, continuing from 1919 into the 1960s, that he was one of the leading writers on popular technology of his generation. A number of very sophisticated projects are described in some detail with good engineering drawings. They include a lightweight flash steam plant for a model aircraft that uses a four cylinder rotary engine, and a fairly accurate steam powered scale model of a Lackawanna RR Pacific engine, in its day (1913) the largest in the world.

There is no sailing model material, but the book is important because it includes a chapter on a radio controlled submarine, eight feet long and with a submerged displacement of 175 pounds. This model, which was completed before the US entered the war in April 1917, is probably the most sophisticated use of radio control by a non-professional before the early 1930s. It is still in the spark and coherer mode, unlike **Miessner** (No 173), but in the design of the synchronised sequence switching devices and in other respects is far in advance of what **Phillips** (No.178, 179) was doing at the same period, and later.

Despite the work's title, the pages carry the running head 'Model Engineering', suggesting a very late change of mind over what the book should be called. The English edition was printed in the USA, with the probable exception of the title page, which is in a slightly different style and carries the English publisher's details on the recto rather than the reverse. An entry in the NYPL *Guide* records that the dust wrapper describes this as an edited collection of articles by various hands collected from *Everyday Engineering*. Given the very wide range of projects covered, this is not unlikely, but we found no reference in the book itself to its being such a compilation.

We have not seen the 1985 reprint, but we assume it is a straightforward re-issue of a work of great historical interest.

THE PERIODICAL SOURCES

These are critical for getting a hold on the history of model yachting. Over the years, they have contained much more, and more varied, material than all the books put together. Though they are still concerned mainly with the design and construction of models and with sailing techniques, their coverage of meeting reports and other day to day events in the sport and their letters columns allow some of the social and contextual setting of the sport to be discerned.

The production of specialist journals for a narrow audience is necessarily a commercially hazardous operation, to which the steady flow of closures, changes of coverage and changes of ownership bears witness. It is very clear from this history that neither in the UK nor in the USA was it possible for a journal devoted solely to model yachting to keep its head above water for more than a very short time. Many of the short lived and narrowly focussed model yachting journals were not run on a commercial basis; they depended on subsidy from their editors, from model yachting authorities or from groups of interested individuals.

More widely based titles, run by commercial publishers, typically aimed to cover the whole of the boat modelling spectrum or incorporated their model sailing coverage into a wider model engineering magazine. Even so, they employed the absolute minimum of permanent staff, and paid their free lance contributors rates well below the union minimum. They depended, and still depend very heavily, on material submitted by their readership. Many who became regular contributors, even editors, had begun by sending in a single article on spec.

The editors, almost without exception, were or had been active in some area of the title's coverage, but in relatively few cases were they model yachtsmen. Thus few had the background to make good any unevenness in the coverage provided by their contributors. The superiority, as journals of record and as aids to the historian, of those magazines that did have the benefit of an active model yachtsman as part of their directing staff cannot be over emphasised.

Despite following a policy of almost completely open access (they generally had to do this to find enough material to fill their pages), many magazines came to depend on a relatively small number of regular contributors. Some of these became in effect part time freelance journalists. The picture of the sport that emerges from the periodicals is thus heavily influenced by the interests of a small minority of writer-participants. The influence of these writers on the development of the sport, together with that of some long serving editors, cannot be overestimated.

This section includes all titles, whether devoted primarily to the sport or not, that are known to have contained significant material on model sailing. It is certainly possible that there is some additional matter to be found in the more obscure boy's journals and in the many general craft magazines that we have not been able to examine, but it is unlikely that it will be of great significance[10].

One group of sources which is not covered here are journals and newsletters produced by and for the members of a single club. At various times and in various places these have flourished, some for several years, but we have been able to examine very few of them. Those we have seen tend to concentrate on race reports, with only very occasional forays into topics of more lasting interest. As they are not only of relatively low interest but also almost inaccessible through the normal research processes, we feel justified in omitting them.

In writing on the more significant and long lasting titles it is not possible to give more than an indication of the range of their coverage. By contrast, the more eccentric and less serious probably receive more comment than they are strictly worth; put this down to the authors' interest in the oddball.

---

[10] Several weeks spent in a fairly superficial examination of the multitude of 19th century journals addressed to 'Boys', ' Youths' or 'Young Gentlemen' proved to be some of the most unproductive and wearing research we have ever been involved in. On the other hand, a decision to cease trawling *The Boy's Own Paper* after 1922 was inadvertently found to be an error when a much later source referred us back to a treatment of the vane gear that appeared there in 1923.

PERIODICALS

199   *Amateur Mechanic*: **London, Cassell: Monthly from 1883.**

This was one of a wide range of popular magazines which Cassell introduced on the back of cheaper printing technology and an increasingly literate population. This one was comparatively short lived and was ultimately replaced by the rather different **Work**. The first year's issues contain, among much else, a series of articles on model yacht construction. Some of this eventually re-appeared in the Cassell's **Work** Handbook **Building Model Boats** (No. 64), and may also have formed part of the basis for the material included in the 'Shipbuilding' section of Cassell's **Book of Outdoor Sports and Indoor Amusements** (No.12)

In the magazine the anonymous author also gives an insight into the attitudes of the model yachtsmen of the time. Though he recognises that

> the importance of owning a model yacht is usually realised at about the same time as the amateur experiences promotion from petticoat to pants,

he emphasises the adult, scientific nature of the sport and the differences between proper model yachts and 'the gaily painted products of the toy shop'. The articles also contain some discussion of design considerations which is lost when they are translated into book form, but nothing on Rating Rules or on steering devices, such as the weighted rudder.

The standard of workmanship proposed is high. Discussing planked construction, the author envisages using $^1/_{16}$ inch planks, but says that it will be difficult to produce a planked hull as light as by carving on the bread and butter method. This implies a very sophisticated carving technique. On the other hand, the guidance on carving a hull suggests thinning the sides down to about $^1/_4$ inch, that is anything but sophisticated and would surely be heavier than a planked hull. Perhaps more than one author was involved, even in this brief series?

200   *Amateur Work, By the Author of Every Man His Own Mechanic*: **London, Ward Lock, weekly, 1881-1884 (seven volumes).**
'New series' 1888-91.
'Complete series' 1881-96.

This must have appeared originally as a part work in weekly numbers, though we have not found it recorded other than in the substantial bound volume form. There is a lively readers' queries section, but it is clear that it was planned from the outset as a systematic coverage of the whole range of home crafts, including practical work in and about the house and garden as well as purely recreational subjects. There are substantial inserts giving detailed patterns for fretwork projects, designs for furniture and the like.

The treatment of model sailing craft is by **Arthur C HIDE**, of whom we have no other knowledge. It is thorough and competent, clearly the work of an experienced builder. He is concerned with models as racing machines, not as scale representation of full size craft, and emphasises the need for accurate preliminary drawings and for following them closely. There are some brief but sensible ideas on how to go about working out a design, but these do not include any element of calculation. The design he himself offers is for a 30 inch loa, straight stemmed cutter of moderate beam with fine ends, 'a type sailed by many model yacht clubs'. His lines plan contains no buttocks or diagonals.

His building technique is bread and butter, with the layers glued up with shellac glue, which he describes as 'linoleum fixing compound, which I believe is made from shellac in spirits of wine'. He aims at a hull wall of $5/8$, heavy for a boat of this size. There is a practical treatment of working out the amount of lead required and the calculation of moments to determine where the CG of the lead should be placed.

His sail plan includes three reduced suits at 90, 80 and 60% of the top suit area, and he advocates the use of completely separate rigs rather than reefing, so he clearly comes from a competitive sailing background. In discussing his choice of sail plan, he prefers the lugger to cutter or schooner, because the sail plan is less divided, giving advantages to windward, and it is fastest on a reach. This suggests that he may have been a member of the club that then sailed on the Serpentine, or at some other club where the typical course was a reach both ways.

The brief treatment of sailing techniques suggests that a beat, a reach and a quartering run can be achieved by the use of sail trim alone. Courses further off the wind call for the use of a weighted rudder, 'which cannot be too heavy'.

AMYA Quarterly:
see *Model Yachting* (No. 234)

201   *Bateau Modèle*: Lyon, J2P Editions: Bi-monthly
        from February 1995.
This journal, which we have not seen, was founded in the Lyon premises of *Modèle Reduit de Bateau* when that title was moved

to Paris. We are told that it gives some coverage to model sailing, particularly to the 1-metre class, but it lacks the space to give a consistent picture.

202 *Beeton's Boy's Monthly Magazine*: **London, Samuel Beeton: Monthly from 1865.**

Sam Beeton, as well as being the spouse and publisher of the more famous Mrs Beeton, published a wide range of journals. This one is aimed at the children of the prosperous middle classes and contains a fair amount of improving 'scientific' writing, as well as the usual fiction.

In the 1865 volume there is a long article on yachting, which seeks to enthuse its audience for a sport that, the writer admits, is outside the reach of any but the wealthy. Though there is some factual material on the number of clubs and yachts and the value of prizes, the main thrust is to extol the sport as bringing men into intimate acquaintance with the sea, 'to which Englishmen, one and all, take naturally'. He emphasises the pure, Corinthian motives of the English yachtsman, 'who sails for pleasure only and is not like the racehorse owner who regards money profit as the first and most indispensable consideration of his sport.'

This is a very different perspective on the attitudes of many owners (both of yachts and horses) from that which we have taken from the history of 19th century yachting and horse racing, where very similar attitudes are found in both groups, whose personnel overlapped to a degree. The only significant difference is the absence from yachting of very obvious and public betting on race results. Private wagers, often large ones, were however very common.

Given the enthusiasm for sailing demonstrated in this contribution, it was inevitable that a model yacht would feature sooner or later. It is perhaps surprising that it took another couple of years before **J J Hissey**, of whom we have no other knowledge, steps forward to instruct the young readers on how to go about it.

His prescriptions are not convincing. The hull is to be carved from a solid block of oak, 'more durable' or pine, 'easier to work'. The interior is to be hollowed first, without any discussion of how the exterior shape might relate to the inside, or indeed to how the exterior shape is to be determined. Everything is very by and large and there are no useful drawings. The spars are to be made of oak 'for strength' and equipped with sails the sizes of which, by contrast, are meticulously specified. The rigging proposals are equally bizarre and there is no discussion of running rigging, sail control, steering or any of the things that need to be done to make the boat actually sail.

In the same volume is a similarly brief article on a simple steam powered model, which is powered by a steam jet, free venting from the boiler into the water at the stern.

203   *The Boy's Journal* **(Edited by Henry VICKERS):**
         London, Monthly from 1863.
         Last issue, February, 1872, subsequently
         combined *with Youth's Play Hour.*

An early boy's monthly, not to be confused with the later, and longer lived, evangelical weekly, **Boy's Own Paper**, which was published by the Religious Tract Society.

It occupies an intermediate position, lying between the weekly sensational literature characterised as 'penny bloods' and the truly improving journals like **Boy's Own Paper** and Routledge's *Every Boy's Magazine*. It has a strong line in adventure serials, many written by Captain Mayne Reid. One, that lies next to the model yachting articles discussed, deals with the sado-masochistic pleasures of colonial expansion, and encompasses both the agonies of capture and torture by slave traders and the fun of wiping them all out in the final episode. Alongside all this, it published in its 1864 volume what are, so far as we can determine, the earliest known designs for specifically model sailing boats, rather than models of full size craft.

The drawings, for a 16 inch lugger and for a cutter to be built at either 18 inches or 36 inches, are very well drawn and the cutter is a handsome and practical design, but the accompanying instructions for building are crude and confusing. There is a follow on piece on rigging and sail making that is equally unsatisfactory, not least because the rigging and other details are still very close to scale imitations of full size practice.

204   *Boys of England*: **(edited by C STEVENS and later**
         by E J BRETT): London, fortnightly from 1866.
This was a fairly long lived boy's journal. It is not clear whether the E J Brett who took over as editor within the first year is the Edwin Brett who wrote an admirable little book on full size sailing, *Notes on Yachts* (London, 1866).

If he was involved with this magazine, he was asleep when the material on model boat building included in the first volume was commissioned. It is brief and superficial. Further articles on the rigging and sailing of the boat were promised but had not appeared by the end of the second year's issues.

The Brett of *Boys of England* was also editor and publisher of a remarkable range of boys journals and collections of cheap fiction for both boys and girls, including The 'Princesses' series of novelettes and titles such as *A Wedding Manual* and *Love Spells and Marriage Forecasts*. A fairly superficial examination of many of his journals has brought to light no material on model sailing, and little to suggest that he could have been the author of *Notes on Yachts*.

205   ***The Boy's Own Paper* (edited originally by J MACAULAY): London, The Religious Text Society, weekly from 1878.**
Last issue, 1967.

A journal offering moral uplift and wholesome recreation to schoolboys, **BOP** carried a steady trickle of material on model sailing craft, starting as early as the second volume with detailed instructions on building, rigging and sailing by O O Ashworth and other material by **H Stansfield Hicks**, tea merchant, philanthropist and active yachtsman and model yachtsman for most of his life (See also No. 136). A number of the regular contributors on other subjects are known to have also been active model yachtsmen.

By Volume 5 (1883), **BOP** is bidding to become a journal of record for the sport, carrying club contact addresses and details of the sailing waters in and around London. It is likely that most of this regular material is contributed by **T E Biddle** (see No. 5), who for a number of years also writes an annual review of the model yachting season. These reviews were taken over at an uncertain date, but not later than 1891, by another hand, probably W J Gordon, a **BOP** regular and author of books on railways, natural history and on morally uplifting subjects, who was a member of the Clapham Model Yacht Club.

The annual reviews contain much succinct history of the sport and information about the measurement Rules and sailing practice of many of the clubs with which the well travelled Biddle is familiar. The first, in 1883, is illustrated by a fine colour lithograph after a water colour by his brother, Capt. R J Biddle, 'the marine artist', which shows models sailing on the Round Pond. At this time T E was a member and R J, Treasurer of the MYSA club at the Round Pond.

After 1884, there is some evidence that this annual review drew on the *Model Yachtsman and Canoeist*, (No. 235), but it also contains much material not to be found elsewhere. Biddle however does not deign to mention of *MY&C*, even in response to a request for sources of lines plans for models.

The detailed coverage and annual reviews cease after 1895. There is little of interest for some years until a report in 1904 on the Junior London MYC by Harold Macfarlane, which emphasises the high seriousness and social exclusiveness of this club for the sons of gentlemen, an offshoot of the London MYC.

This apart, the model yachting content is feeble for many years and in 1907 a competition for the best carved model hull attracts no entries, when other competitions, even those for verse writing, attract hundreds. This told the editor something, and in 1920 he repeats, word for word and diagram for diagram, the articles by Ashworth that had been used forty years earlier. There is no further serious model yacht material, apart from a design by H Hambley Tregonning in 1924 that includes details of his masthead vane gear that also features in **Bauduin's** book. (No. 8).

In 1924, the pseudonymous author of a long running series on building various types of home wireless receiver offered a home built wireless control set for a model boat. He envisages an electrically powered model four feet long and his design is for a spark gap and coherer system, similar to that used by **Phillips** in 1912 (See No.177). Subsequent 'replies to readers' suggest that some attempts to construct such a set were being made.

206   ***Buenas Amuras* (edited by Juan Miguel ROIG):**
         Buenos Aires, CAYM, irregular from August 1983.
         From 1993, annually in December.

This small, but persistent, journal is the house magazine of the Club Argentino de Yatemodelismo, the Argentine national authority. It is clearly produced under some difficulty, but usually contains brief reports of the more important international regional and local regattas, CAYM social events and small amounts of technical information. As Juan is an English speaker, he goes to some trouble to keep his readers *au fait* with what is going on in the wider world of model yachting, both in Europe and in the USA, including some book reviews and reports of ISAF-RSD business.

207   ***The Captain, a Magazine for Boys and Old Boys*:**
         London, weekly from 1899.
         last issue, 1924.

As the title indicates, a boy's paper aimed specifically at the public schools. In this it differed from the *Boy's Own Paper* which, though initially aimed at much the same market, was more widely read and after a few years made specific efforts to cover the interests of non public school readers.

114

Along with the usual run of boy's fiction, *The Captain* gives extended coverage to public school sport, especially cricket. We have not examined all the volumes, but we have found little hobby centred material and nothing specifically on model yachting except a brief article in 1912 by E W Hobbs, the founding Secretary of the MYRA. This is the first appearance in print of the organisation, founded the previous year, and the only surviving record of the results of what were probably the first MYRA national championships, held in 1912.

English Mechanic, English and Amateur Mechanics, see Work (No. 249).

208   *Every Boys Hobby Annual*: London, Fleetway Publications, annually from 1926 to 1938.

A compendium, mainly of practical construction projects, aimed at the readers of the Harmsworth weekly journal *The Modern Boy* and at the children of *Daily Mail* readers. In appearance and general content, it is similar to *The Modern Boy*, though with a higher proportion of practical construction articles. Every volume has railway and aircraft modelling, fretwork, woodworking and home wireless receiver construction items. Model boats appear less frequently, usually in alternate years, and all the contributions are aimed at simple boats that a boy might reasonably build for himself.

The contributions are anonymous, but include E W Hobbs and George Colman Green, who can each be identified from internal evidence. With one exception all the material on sailing models is competent and sensible. Hobbs' pieces in the 1927 and 1928 issues is very similar to what he had written in the *Harmsworth's Household Encyclopaedia*, (No. 66), also published by Fleetway. Green's boat of 1933 is described as 'fitting into the 36 inch class approved by the Imperial Junior League'. It offers evidence that he thought the League's schoolboy members should be capable of carving a bread and butter hull that would end up with a ballast ratio of 55%, and of making a Braine gear of sorts.

209   *Every Boy's Magazine* (edited by Edward ROUTLEDGE): London, Routledge, monthly from 1862.

from 1865, as *Routledge's Magazine for Boys.*

from 1869, as *The Young Gentleman's Magazine.*

from 1874, reverts to *Every Boy's Magazine.*

incorporated into *Boy's Own Paper*, 1889.

Regardless of the successive changes in title, the annual bound sets were sold under the title *Routledge's Every Boy's Annual.*

Routledge ran a seriously intentioned journal with which he avowedly sought to counteract the influence of the proprietors of 'penny bloods' who he characterised as 'men of intelligence, who are engaged in disseminating sensational literature and crude opinions, highly injurious to the healthy training and indisputably destructive of the opening germs of the youthful mind'. He set out his aims in an article addressed to parents and guardians rather than to his boy readers, in which he said that juvenile journals must seek two things, 'first, attractiveness, second, utility'.

To this end, while not eschewing the adventure stories that are the staple of boys' journals, he carried a much higher proportion of improving and factual material, including supplements covering public school sporting activity and regular prize competitions for written and artistic work, models and the like. There were long and very competent series on 'Tools and their Uses' and 'Our Workshop', both by Temple Thorold, who also took the readers through the construction of a stationary steam engine and a model locomotive of considerable complexity and sophistication.

In 1865, the magazine carried a couple of articles on model yacht building by **W H G Kingston**, which expand on the brief instructions given in his *Boy's Book of Boats* (No. 84). The instruction is quite detailed, and reference is made to 'the model yacht club that sails on the Serpentine', 'where the boats can be made to sail on any desired course', but Kingston is here concerned to produce a model **of** a yacht, rather than a model yacht. He makes only minimal concessions to the needs of a practical model, particularly in respect of the rigging.

The boat proposed is a 30 inch long cutter, to be carved from a single block. Though he clearly knows what he is doing, Kingston reveals himself as far removed from the practice of competitive model yachtsmen, even at this relatively early date. The construction is heavy and much of the ballast is carried internally. There is almost total reproduction of the fittings, standing and running rigging of a full size yacht, even down to reef points and ensign halyards.

The description of the physics of sailing is interesting, rather than helpful, and of course shows no awareness of the role of pressure differential in generating the propulsive force. Similarly the discussion of the balancing of the rig is convoluted and hard to follow, partly because he does not use the concepts of CLR and CE, partly because he seeks to adjust the balance only by the relative trim of the foresails. Only as a throwaway conclusion, does he suggest that the sails may need to be reefed, or the trim of the hull adjusted to get an effective balance. Though his model is fitted with a rudder, he advises against trying to use it, as 'models must perforce be steered by the trim of the sails'. There is no discussion of even the most elementary automatic steering.

We have not examined the whole run of this title. It is quite likely, given its strong practical element, that other contributions on model sailing will have been carried over its long life.

210   *The Field, the Gentleman's Magazine*: **London, Horace Cox, weekly from 1853.**
This wide ranging magazine aimed, at least up to the First World War, to cover all the gentlemanly sports with authority and in some detail, but did not regularly cater to model yachtsmen. Nonetheless, gentlemen who were in the habit of using it as a vehicle for discussion of their full size sailing, also write occasionally about their models.

For instance it carries the earliest report of an international model yacht race, that held at Birkenhead in 1853, and there are occasional designs and discussions of design concepts. These tend to come in bursts, as one contribution will spark off ripostes and controversy from other readers. This is evidence that significant numbers of model sailers, most of them by no means country gentlemen and with no pretensions to owning a full size yacht, were regular readers of the journal. In 1884 there is an extended correspondence about the problem of 'running off' in models; all the writers are already known as contributors and correspondents to *The Model Yachtsman and Model Yacht Club Reporter.*

211   *Forest and Stream*: New York, Forest and Stream
Publishing Co., weekly from 1873, monthly from
1915, ceased publication 1930.

This American sporting magazine covered a very wide range of
gentlemanly sports, and appears to have been similar to *The Field*
(No. 210) in its aims, though more forward looking in its early use
of extensive photographic illustration. It did not give regular
coverage to model yachting, but carried occasional articles. All that
we have seen deal with the sailing of the American MYC, that
operated on the lake in Prospect Park, Brooklyn. In March 1894
there was a piece with several photos of representative boats and
in November the same year a short series on model yacht building.
This includes the lines of *Neola,* a boat to the American MYC Rule
and illustrations of steering gear that also appear somewhat later
in **Fisher**'s book (No. 46). There is also detail of the sailing and
competition Rules used for skiff sailing at Prospect Park. A later
article in 1924 has good photos of boats and skiffs in action.

212   *Hunt's Yachting Magazine*: London, Hunt,
Monthly, from August, 1852:
last issue, 1879.

Hunt was the first to devote a journal specifically to the yachting
community, also publishing his annual *Universal Yacht List* from
1853. This last continued, in various forms, well into the twentieth
century. The *Yachting Magazine* survived with some difficulty in
competition with more general sporting magazines such as *The
Field* and *Bell's Life*, and with other short lived yachting titles.

During its early years it was pleased to carry contributed
material on model yachting to fill out its pages. The first few
volumes carry useful scraps of information about early model yacht
clubs, often from before the foundation of the magazine. There is
also more extended coverage of the conflicts within the London
MYC, which includes a complete copy of the club's constitution and
sailing and rating rules, as well as some information on their
sailing practice.

There is no treatment of construction methods and no
illustrations relating to models. In response to a reader's request,
the editor regrets he is not competent to describe the construction
of models, but will be pleased to publish on the topic, if some expert
will write. No one offers.

The coverage of model matters tapers away after about 1857
and we have not examined the later volumes after 1860.

213   *Junior Mechanics and Electricity*: London,
Percival Marshall, fortnightly from 1913
From 1924, as *The Mechanical Boy*.

Last issue, 1925.

This was initially a version of **Model Engineer** aimed at schoolboys. The content at the outset is very similar to **ME**, though slightly less demanding of tools and skill levels. In its eleven years of life we have found only one substantial article on model yachting. This is by Bill Daniels and gives a drawing and construction notes for a 24 inch model yacht. This, in 1914, has a bermuda rig, one of the very first, if not the first, to be seen on a published model design. There is also, in a reply to a reader in March 1913, a lines plan that is in fact a reduced size version of Daniels' 12-metre *Substitute* that appeared in the 1913 edition of *Model Sailing Yachts* (No. 95).

There is very little further model yachting material while the title remains **Junior Mechanics**, though there is a very small amount in **The Mechanical Boy**.

     Marine Models
     see *The Model Yachtsman* (No. 234)

214   *Marine Modelling*: Upton on Severn, Traplet
Publishing, bi-monthly from October 1985.

from October, 1988, monthly.

from May 1990, edited by Chris JACKSON.
from June 1998, as *Marine Modelling*
International.

A general boat modelling magazine, one of a stable of model magazines run by Traplet in competition with the group under the Nexus banner. It has a smaller circulation than **Model Boats**, but a higher proportion of readers overseas, particularly in the USA.

Since Chris Jackson took over as editor he has sought to differentiate it from its rival by continuing to emphasise the 'how to do it' tradition of this sort of hobby magazine. Reflecting his own background in the sport, there is a reasonable amount of model yachting material, including practical articles on modern construction methods and a small but valuable series of designs to the principal model yacht classes, including one or two vintage designs from the 1930s. There is also some, though still slight, material from overseas.

The Mechanical Boy.
see *Junior Mechanics (No. 213).*

215   *Modelist-Konstructor*: **Moscow, Monthly from 1970**
Initially, a very wide ranging popular mechanics type of journal with material on radio and television maintenance, DIY projects and the like, as well as a small amount of model building,. We have seen only a few tear sheets from the early 1970's containing plans for radio controlled Marbleheads. One is an unacknowledged copy, even to its original mini-gaff rig, of Roger Stollery's *March Hare.*

In more recent years, the subject matter has been largely model oriented, with the emphasis on scale models of aircraft and power boats. Backing this has been material on full size developments, for instance a long and excellent series on the technical history of the steam torpedo boats of the latter part of the last century.

The very small amount of sail oriented material in more recent issues tends to deal with experimental and non-standard types of boat rather than with competitive model yachts. This suggests that there may now be a separate title covering the interests of competitive skippers and designers, which we have not been able to locate.

216   *Model Boating World News*: **US Journal, no publication detail available.**
Last issue early 1970s
We have seen no issues of this journal, but we understand that it contained the first regular series of articles on radio sailing published in the US. These ran from the late 1960s until the magazine's demise under the title 'Tiller Talk'. They were mainly written by Ray Hottinger, with some contributions from **Rod Carr.**

Model Boats
see *Model Maker* (No. 221)

217   *Model Builder* **(edited by William NORTHROP):
Costa Mesa, CA, Model Builder Magazine Co.,
Monthly from early 1970s?**

This US magazine had a wide remit, but in our context is
principally important for carrying 'Strictly Sail', an irregular series
of general articles on radio yachting by Rod Carr, a long time radio
sailor and sailmaker, from 1971 to 1978. These cover a wide range
of topics, from design concepts and construction tips to sail trim
and race tactics. Much of it is of only ephemeral interest, but it
gives a good impression of the early days of organised radio sailing
in the US, as the AMYA was getting itself organised. Rod
subsequently transferred his writings to *US Boat and Ship
Modeller* (No. 248)

218   *Model Craftsman* **(edited by E STIERI): New York,
Emanuele Stieri, Monthly from March 1933.
from August 1933, Chicago**

from October 1934, East Stroudsberg, PA

from March 1935, publisher is Charles Penn

from August, 1942, Ramsey NJ.

from May, 1950 as *RailRoad Model Craftsman*

We have been unable to locate a run of this title in the UK and the
description is supplied by one of our informants.

This magazine set out originally to provide a wide coverage of
model engineering and other cognate topics and had some well
known model yachtsmen associated with its original editorial team;
most of these, however, left after a few months. Its model yachting
material was sporadic and patchy, but in its early years included a
number of designs by Thomas Darling and others, many of them
for classes that were not at that time recognised by MYRAA. In the
late 1930s there are a number of designs for the Marblehead class,
including Archie Arroll's *Detroit News*, and short pieces by Roy
Clough on the origins and virtues of the class.

The late 1930s sees the most regular model yachting coverage
and in 1940-41 it contains the series of articles on plank-on-frame
construction by Charles Farley that appeared again in 1945 in
MYRAA's *Model Yachting* (No. 233) and again in 1996 as a
USVMYG reprint (No. 35). Once the US entered the war, model
yachting coverage becomes sporadic and seems to have ceased
entirely in August 1945, at the time the magazine was re-orienting
itself as a predominantly model railway magazine. This change
occurred some time before it formally became the *RailRoad*

Model Craftsman. Despite this, it advertised itself to model yachtsmen in a panel in the MYRAA journal *Model Yachting* during 1945-46 as 'the old faithful', suggesting that it had not entirely given up hopes of attracting readers and authors interested in sailing craft.

219   **Model Engineer: London, Percival Marshall, monthly from 1898.**

various titles in its early years, e. g. *Model Engineer and Home Electrician, ME and Light Machinery Review.*

from Sept 1900, fortnightly.

from December 1902, weekly.

Many other titles incorporated over the years, e.g. *Home Mechanics* in 1959.

Percival Marshall absorbed into Model and Allied Press in 1965; for subsequent publishing history, see *Model Maker* (No. 221).

ME was the origin and backbone of Percival Marshall's large scale publishing activity, almost all of which was aimed at the needs of gentleman amateur engineers and model makers. Initially the magazine contained no model yachting material, probably because it was thought too far from the mechanical engineering and home generation of electricity that were its main topics in the early years. But towards the end of its first year, in discussing the possibility of a club for model engineers, Marshall remarked that 'Model yachtsmen ... have long organised themselves into clubs.'

You can almost see the light come on over his head as he realises that there is an untapped segment of the market that might be persuaded to buy *ME*. In the following issue he announces the institution of a model yachting supplement to be carried once a month and invites his readers to contribute. Initially the space is filled by club secretaries retailing the history of their clubs, but soon it becomes a valuable, if patchy, record of serious model yachting activity. The first flush of model yachting coverage subsides quite quickly into a very tedious controversy over the merits of conflicting Rating Rules.

The coverage waxes and wanes over the years, with valuable material by Daniels appearing in the years up to 1914 and during the 1914-18 war. This raises the question of what Daniels (who was of military age) did during the war. Model yachting coverage reaches a peak in the 1920s, when H B Tucker, then Chairman of the reconstituted Model Yachting Association, edited the monthly yachting pages as a more or less independent entity. There is full coverage of the MYA's activity and of the annual competitions for the *Yachting Monthly* Cup, as well as weighty contributions on design from Alfred Turner and others. A small number of designs are carried, but they tend to be important ones by Daniels and Turner.

By 1928 Tucker reckoned the market was strong enough to support a separate monthly devoted to model yachting and left to found *Model Yachtsman*. After this date *ME*'s coverage withers and there is little further of interest until after 1945, when very occasional articles on radio control of yachts appear.

220   **The Modelmaker: New York, Spon and Chamberlain,: Monthly, from January 1924: In 1935 transferred to Wauwatosa WI, The Modelmaker Corporation (a subsidiary of Kalmbach Inc.) : periodicity changed to nine issues a year:**

last issue, October, 1940(?).

Combined with *The Model Craftsman*, Ramsey NJ, Model Craftsman Publications, monthly from December, 1940.

This was at the outset a slim, small format monthly that sought to cover the whole range of model engineering and model making. It was a pale imitation of Percival Marshall's *Model Engineer*, and assumed that most of its readers were also subscribers to the British magazine. Though its more mainstream model engineering coverage includes designs and construction features, there is little of this type of material in its slight coverage of model yachting. This consists mainly of nearly meaningless reports of club racing. The boats that are discussed in any detail are small, under 30 inches and the only design offered is for a 24 lwl boat.

There are also some more interesting reports on children's regattas organised by school boards or local community organisations and sponsored by local newspapers. That in Los Angeles in 1925 attracted over 250 entrants from schools within the County school board area.

For a long period from 1929 to 1939 there is no coverage of sailing craft, as the magazine re-orients itself as a model railroad and power boat magazine. After its take-over by the Kalmbach company, this trend is reinforced, and its sub title is changed to emphasise model engineering, which the editor regards as 'involving design, construction and problem solving, just as in full size engineering'. The page size, number of pages and quality of production are much improved in the late 1930s.

In 1939-40, model yachting returns in regular form, with a monthly column by C O Brook, regular contributions from Charles Farley, then Chairman of the MYRAA, articles on fittings and on sail plan design. There are also some designs, including an A boat by Fred L Pidgeon, specifically for the lighter wind condition found in the US and a modelised version of the Star keel boat by J R Many.

No sooner had this valuable model yachting strand become established than the magazine was merged with *The Model Craftsman*. (No. 218). and it faded away to almost nothing.

221   *Model Maker, incorporating Model Mechanic and Model Cars*: 'New series, monthly from July 1950', Leicester, The Drysdale Press.
Various title changes

1961-4, *Model Maker and Model Cars.*

1965, *Model Maker and Model Boats,*

From August 1965 as *Model Boats.*

Various changes of location and publisher:

from January, 1952, Watford, Model Aeronautical Press.

from 1965, Hemel Hempstead, from June, 1968, Model and Allied Publications.

from May, 1986, Argus Specialist Publications;

from January, 1995, Nexus Specialist Publications.

from mid 1998, Swanley, Nexus Specialist Publications.

This long and continuing sequence of publications under various titles and ownership is the pre-eminent, if less than fully satisfactory, source for the history of model yachting in the UK since 1945. The coverage of the sport fluctuates over the years and depends very heavily on what is contributed from the field. The first few years are relatively sparse, but with the arrival of **Vic Smeed** as assistant editor in 1952 (and later as editor), the model boating content, and with it the model yachting element, increases, aided by the spinning off of radio modelling and model cars to separate titles.

There were several substantial series on the design process and on construction. Many of the more important of these eventually became books in their own right. The reporting of the results of major events is less than complete and, in many cases, little more than a results sheet with little or no discussion of their significance.

For the historian, the most important role of the magazine over the years has been the publication of designs for each of the major classes. For many years the way a designer made some money from his work was by selling his design to the Plans Service run by the magazine. Each addition was marked by a reduced size publication in the magazine, usually accompanied by explanatory text from the designer. The quality of these brief articles varies, but collectively they are the best record of the aims and ideas of designers over a period of some forty years.

The introduction and widespread popularity of radio controlled racing, has increased the commercial attraction of selling successful designs in kit form. This has meant that the number of designs offered to magazines in this way has fallen away and the magazine has to all intents ceased to provide designs for the competitive skipper. More important, it has largely ceased to be a forum for the discussion of design ideas. Recently the company disposed of much of its 'back list' of plans to an independent supplier[11]. From his lists it looks as though many have been lost in the transfer.

Similarly, wider changes in the boat modelling scene and (possibly) the predilections of the current editor, have meant that a large part of the magazine is now made up of regular columns. These often too closely reflect the month by month activity of the individual writers and contain relatively little information on design, construction or operation of practical value to the reader or to subsequent historians.[12] Detailed 'how to do it' articles still appear, but relatively seldom on model yachting topics.

---

[11] X-List Plans, 22 Old Brewery Close, Aylesbury, Bucks, HP21 7SH
[12] I have to confess that I have been, for long periods, one of these columnists, but plead that the *Curved Air* column from time to time contained substantial information on aspects of the history of the sport, reflecting the progress of my own work. RP.

222   *Model Mechanic*, (edited by G H DEASON):
      **Leicester, The Drysdale Press, monthly from May,
      1946.**
      Bi-monthly from mid 1950.
      Last issue, September/October, 1950.

A short lived venture by the Drysdale Press, which published a range of other modelling and crafts titles. This one covered nearly all forms of modelling except model aircraft and, as model sailing was very slow to resume organised competition after the war, its model yachting material is sparse. It does not attempt to record the activity of the Model Yachting Association, which, so far as it is covered, is to be found in the competing **Marine and Aero Models**. (No. 236)

Much of what it does carry on sailing is made up of generalities on the history of the Rating Rules and what makes a good Rule, together with speculative treatments of new ideas that had yet to be brought to fruition, including the use of bulbous bows for the control of wave making and the possibility of fleet racing under radio control. In its brief life, only two designs for class yachts are offered, for the Marblehead *Merlin* by L A Garrett, and for the 36R *Lady Betty* by 'A Shipwright', but actually Bernard Reeves. The series of articles on the building and fitting out of this last was incomplete when the title was merged with *Model Cars* and was eventually completed in the early issues of *Model Maker*.

223   *Le Modèle Reduit de Bateau*: **Paris, Publications
      MRA: later, Lyon, Publications MRA: quarterly
      from Summer 1942;
      bi-monthly from May-June, 1947; monthly
      from January, 1981:**

      from 1994, Paris, WEKA Presse

      from 1997, Paris, Rigel Editions.

This long lived French language title has covered all aspects of marine modelling for over fifty years. Naturally, its coverage of model yachting has varied in quantity and quality over this time, but, as it has been for most of this time the sole French language vehicle, it has frequently contained useful material.

It had a particularly rich period in the 1980s, when the editor was one of the leading competitive skippers in France and he and his colleagues on the circuit published a number of valuable discussions of the development of radio sailing in France and of their individual design odysseys. After he left, the model yachting content was reduced.

The magazine went through a series of changes of ownership, during which it fell into the doldrums, before being stabilised under the ownership of Rigel, which has brought a return to a steady, if limited, diet of high quality technical writing on model yachting. The magazine's plans service has, over the years, published a series of important boats by the leading French designers in each generation.

224   *Model Ships and Power Boats*: **London, Percival Marshall, monthly from January 1948:**

last issue, December 1953.

Continued as *Ships and Ship Models*: London, Percival Marshall, monthly from January 1954 incorporated into *Model Engineer*, April, 1959.

When *MSPB* started publication, it announced itself as a partial replacement for *Ships and Ship Models*, a Marshall title that had run from 1931 to the outbreak of war in 1939. *SSM* had not covered model yachting, but the new venture announced its intention to do so and did carry some material of interest. There was a plans service that included a series of yacht plans by A W Littlejohn, including the 36R *Penguin* and the 'M' *Falcon*.

Unfortunately the magazine publication of these was in the form of a sail plan only, so it is not now possible to access the lines. The only plan from which it would be possible to build is a 36R by F C Tansley, by then the Commodore of the club at Hove. The design dated from 1938, but was still racing successfully when the lines were published in the magazine in 1950.[13]

Tansley also wrote some good articles summarising design development in the various classes. These offer information not to be found elsewhere, and good photos of representative boats back to the turn of the century. He wrote a further series on the model yachting history of his family, who had been active since the middle of the last century. Again, illustrated with family snaps that give an impression of the atmosphere of model yachting in his home town of Lowestoft in the 1890s.

There are also articles by **C E Bowden** on his experiments with wing sails and on his approach to radio control of model yachts. These anticipate the material that appears in the later

---

18 This design, *Skylark II*, was re-published in June 1999 by ***Marine Models International***, and is now available from the Traplet Plans Service.

editions of his book, (No.9) and are important because Bowden is one of the first to approach radio control in model yachts as a user, rather than a radio experimenter. His controversies with the radio experts over the way forward focus the discussion for the next decade or so.

225   *The Model Yacht*: **Nominally monthly, but with some gaps, from September 1928. Combined with** *Model Yachting* **(No. 227) in December 1929.**

This US magazine had only a brief independent existence, being absorbed by *Model Yachting*. We have not seen any issues.

226   *The Model Yacht* **(edited by Earl BOEBERT): Albuquerque, NM, US Vintage Model Yacht Group, by subscription: Three issues a year, from Spring 1997.**

This is the organ of the USVMYG and borrows its title from one and title page illustration from another journal of the 1930s (Nos. 225 and 232). As well as day to day administrative matters, it includes increasing amounts of competent 'how to do it' material and many issues carry as an appendix a reprint of a vintage design, taken from earlier publications. Its content reflects the much higher proportion of USVMYG membership who have a competitive background in the sport than is the case in the UK based counterpart organisation. The USVMYG is also beginning to make available a range of plans from earlier American designers, and to republish some of the classic texts from the past (see No. 45).

227   *Model Yachting* **(edited by Arthur R Brown): Melrose Highlands, MA: monthly from January 1929. from December 1929, combined with** *The Model Yacht* **as** *Model Yachting and the Model Yacht.*

The *National Union Catalogue* reports that this title absorbed a previous journal, *The Model Yacht*, in December 1929, but the numbering of the only issue that we have seen suggests that it was first published in January 1932. We have seen only the last issue of April 1934, which is a very slight production, of little interest.

228   *Modellbau Heute*: Berlin, Zentalvorstand der
       Gesellschaft fûr Sport und Technik, Monthly from
       1970.

This was the organ of the DDR's state organisation for model sports and gave coverage to model aircraft, power boats and model cars as well as sailing models.

We have seen only recent issues and, from the time of the DDR, only a single copy from 1988 and a few tear sheets of plans from the 1970s and eighties. So far as we can judge from the small sample we have seen, the emphasis at that time was on competition within each of the areas covered.

The 1988 copy also has extensive reporting of the political speeches from the platform at the GST's 30th annual congress. It was addressed by the General who was then the DDR's Minister for Defence, who awarded the Karl-Marx-Order to the GST for its services to the republic. A profile of a leading model yachtsman, Siegfried Wagner, emphasises his role as a leader of the model sailing section of the 'Maxim Gorky' *Pionierhaus* in his home town of Sömmerda and the retinue of keen young model yachtsmen he has built up round him.

Despite this strong political emphasis, and some photos illustrating early post war model flying in the DDR that have a distinct air of 1930s 'Strength through Joy' propaganda, the reporting of current activity is reassuringly similar to what was to be found in Western journals of the same period, even to the hairstyles of the younger participants. Technically, the model yachting activity seems very much on a par with what was going on in Britain at the same time. The plans that are advertised as available from the magazine include no model yachts, though they published at least two radio M designs in issues in 1978 and 1983. Curiously, these are both by the Hungarian Istvan Toth. One of them is the well known *Flipper,* widely sailed in Germany in the late sixties and seventies. This design is another unacknowledged copy of one of Stollery's 'tubular' boats of the mid sixties.

Despite the collapse of the DDR and the GST, the magazine continued as a commercial enterprise and now devotes itself almost entirely to scale modelling from plastic kits.

228 **Modelcraft Magazine (edited by H S COLEMAN): London, Modelcraft Ltd. Quarterly from January 1947. Last issue 1955?**

Modelcraft was a company founded by Coleman in the late 1930s; it produced a range of plans and 'Planbooks' (largely for static 'galleon' type models) and booklets on a wider range of projects. These continued through the war in the face of considerable difficulty after his premises were bombed, but Coleman was driven by an almost religious belief in the value of modelling both for the individual and for the wider society.

The magazine seems to have been started as soon after the war as he could get an allocation of paper. The early issues are curious; they consist of quarterly re-issues of the company's catalogue (unchanged at each issue except for a small insert on new products) with a small amount of editorial matter wrapped round it. This suggests that Coleman may have been using a paper allocation, granted for the production of a trade catalogue, in ways that the Board of Trade had not really intended.

It has to be said that the catalogue is in some ways more interesting than the magazine proper. At the outset it offered 18 plans for galleons and other static models, 50 or more for $1/50$ scale waterline models of warships together with $1/50$ and $1/100$ plans for merchant vessels of various types. Other ranges included military vehicle plans, $1/72$ scale aircraft plans and some small flying models. Apart from the model railway plans, mainly for buildings and lineside features, everything is of fairly limited ambition. This reflects the austerities of a list built up during war-time restrictions and Coleman's desire to reach the young with the joys of modelling.

On the model yachting front, Modelcraft offered plans for boats at 9 inches (this is just possibly the design included in Coleman's book, No, 45), 18 inches and 24 inches. This last is to be built by bread and butter techniques and is equipped with Braine gear. These are in addition to Bernard Reeves' 1943 Planbook for a cardboard model yacht (No. 118).

In support of these small designs the company offered a pack of fittings in brass, complete with bowsies and rigging wire, 'suitable for boats up to 36 inches long'. In 1947 this cost £1-1-0 (£1.05), a considerable sum when four sheets of yacht plan were only three shillings and sixpence (£0.17).

Though other parts of the range expand over time, with the addition of more plans and, eventually, a range of kits, there are only two significant additions to the model yachting range. In mid

1948, there is a plan for a boat to the 36R class, (which came with lines and a set of templates for the bread and butter lifts) and a set of lines for a Marblehead. These cost eight shillings and sixpence (£0.43) and 13 shillings and sixpence (£0.68) respectively.

In 1950, a reader survey showed that road vehicles and model railways were by far the most popular topics, and that demand was for kits rather than plans for scratch building. After this there were no additions to the model yacht product range and the slight amount of yachting material in the magazine ceases, with the exception of a highly speculative article in 1951 on the possibilities of radio controlled yachting. This is written by Coleman, who seems to have had full size sailing experience, but, we suspect, had never seen a radio controlled model and possibly was not familiar with model yachting in any form.

In 1955, **Reeves'** book was still in print, but swamped by no less than eight (extremely sound) volumes on model railway techniques by Edward Beal, in his day a highly respected pioneer of realistic railway modelling.

*229 *modell-yacht-info* **(edited originally by Horst KRÖNKE): Niendorf/Ostsee, Vereinigung der Modell-Yacht-Segler e.V., Quarterly from the mid 1980s, possibly with some gaps.**

Later, edited by Gerd Mentges and published from Wedel

This was started by Horst Krönke in imitation of *Model Yachting News* (No. 231) and has grown into the house journal of the German competitive circus. It is largely taken up with regatta reports, ranking lists and the minutiae of Rule variations that necessarily concern such a group. There are occasional pieces on design ideas.

There is an associated title, *RC acktuell*, which we have not seen and on which we cannot comment.

230 *Model Yacht Racing*: **(edited by Carroll F SWEET Jr.) Grand Rapids, MI, monthly from April 1935. Last issue December 1935.**

We have seen only two issues of this magazine, for September and October 1935. It is an eight page production, printed on art paper and with a card cover given over largely to advertisements for forthcoming meetings and for blueprints. The contents include a report on Sam Berge's victory in the *Yachting Monthly* Cup in Fleetwood at the end of the previous month and on recent meetings in the USA. The October issue contains a report and drawing of the vane gear that Berge used on his boat; this apart, there is not much there, apart from race reports. The USVMYG check list of the Houk archive shows that it appeared monthly, but only until December 1935.

*231   *Model Yachting News* (edited by Chris JACKSON): Maylandsea, Jackson, quarterly by subscription from March 1980.

Last issue *MYN*, No. 47, April 1993.

Continued as *Radio Yachting News*, from June 1993 with new numbering from 1.

Various changes of location;

from December, 1981, South Norwood,

from December, 1984, Reigate,

from September, 1994, Nailsea,

last issue, *RYN*, No. 12, March 1996.

This little magazine was run from one man's back bedroom, but aimed squarely at an international audience of seriously competitive model yachtsmen, reflecting the growth of the sport under the influence of radio control. At its peak, it had a circulation of about 1000 world wide and reached subscribers in 26 countries. Given that its world-wide potential audience of competitive skippers cannot have been much more than 5000, its market penetration was impressive, if barely sufficient to make it commercially viable.

It gave a regular slice of its space to the Model Yachting Association, so that the association could communicate directly with its members and for much of its later life it was also the official organ of the International Model Yacht Racing Union.

Its content included major international race results, frequently with technical analysis of the designs involved, designs for fittings, together with regular surveys of available boats, fittings and other equipment. There were very occasional construction features and a number of high quality contributions on aspects of the design process.

From issue four there is an increasing proportion of contributions from outside the UK. From issue five, there is a regular sequence of designs for the main international classes, both published by the magazine as part of its own plans service and as a means of drawing attention to designs available from other sources, often direct from the designer. Over the 16 years of its life the magazine published close on 70 designs. Many of these were contributed from overseas and in this *MYN* made good to some extent the falling away of design content in the long established *Model Boats*. Photo illustrations of good quality are a feature of all but the earliest issues.

In all, it is a valuable record of the concerns of competitive skippers over a period of rapid change in the sport, with close attention paid to the development of the relevant technologies.

After Chris took up the post of editor of the commercial magazine *Marine Modelling*, the magazine was closed down briefly, re-opened, and finally ceased publication in 1996. Its concerns continue, albeit considerably diluted, in *Marine Modelling*.

The success of this venture spawned a French language version, *Voile Modèle Information*, run jointly by Jackson and a French collaborator. This ran to only two quarterly issues in 1988 before being abandoned.

232   *Model Yachting*: **(Edited by Arthur R Brown)**
         Monthly from January 1931: Melrose Highlands
         MA, Print-Craft.

A very slight publication, only 12 small pages a month, but the official organ of MYRAA. It offered a number of blueprints of designs by leading figures of the day, but only for the international 'A' Class and for Marbleheads. The only issue we have seen, that for April 1934, includes a directory of 47 affiliated clubs and details of forthcoming events. The rest is made up of casual gossip and heavy handed humour. Tiny snippets of information can be gleaned from the letters page. Other issues must have been better than this for it to have survived as long as it did.

*233   *Model Yachting: A Monthly Magazine for the*
Miniature Boat Enthusiast **(edited initially by**
Charles FARLEY): Providence RI, All States
Publishing House: monthly, from April 1945.
From February 1950, as *Model Yachting*
Monthly, Sail and Power.

Various changes of editor, location and
publisher'

Frequency drops to bi monthly in June-July
1950, last issue, Aug-September, 1950.

This was the official journal of MYRAA in the post-war period and
represents another failed attempt by the US model yachting
community to produce a journal devoted entirely to model yachting.
Though it survived for five years, it was always a marginal
proposition and struggled to attract enough subscriptions. There is
some evidence that it was directly subsidised by MYRAA and
possibly also by interested individuals. When these subsidies dried
up, a brief attempt was made to attract additional readers by
covering power boats also, but it was soon abandoned.

The content is very variable, with some important designs
being published, and useful discussion of design trends in the US,
particularly the 'finless fin' concepts of Gus Lassel and the use of
the sliding rig. There is good coverage of developments in vane
design with some excellent exploded drawings. Overall, though, it
gives a sad picture of an organisation struggling to keep its troops
together in the face of the expansion of alternative leisure
activities. Its efforts were not helped by divisions in the ranks
between those who wanted to pursue the advances in performance
offered by mechanical aids such as vane gear and sliding rigs, and
those who wanted to outlaw them and freeze the sport in its 1930s
configuration.

In 1949 the editor proposed to the British MYA that it should
cover activity on both sides of the Atlantic and suggested that this
could be achieved if the MYA undertook to take a minimum of 600
copies of each issue. The MYA regarded this as 'unworkable'. There
is no indication of what the US circulation was at that stage.

*234   *Model Yachting*: Various US locations, The
American Model Yachting Association, quarterly
from 1970.
Originally as *AMYA Quarterly*.

This is the current house organ of the AMYA. Because the
Association is organised on an individual membership basis, rather
than as a grouping of clubs, the magazine goes to all its members
as part of the membership package. This guarantees it a
sufficiently large circulation to prosper. It is very largely taken up
with administrative matters and race reports, but has over the
years included some useful constructional and sail making
instruction as well as ideas for gadgets and radio installations.
Until the formation of the US Vintage Model Yacht group as a
Special Interest Group within the AMYA, it has been solely
concerned with radio racing and even now there is little other than
administrative contributions from the USVMYG, whose more
lasting material is found in their own journal *The Model Yacht*
(No. 226). There have been a very small number of plans published
in the journal, most of them for the US 1-metre class.

Originally a small and modestly produced journal, it is now in
large format, glossy and extensively illustrated.

*235   *The Model Yachtsman and Model Yacht Club
Reporter*: Kingston upon Hull, Grassam: Monthly,
from March 1884.
from Jan 1885, as *The Model Yachtsman and
Canoeing Gazette*.

From January, 1885, as *The Model Yachtsman
and Canoeist*.

Last issue, November 1894.

This is the first specialist magazine devoted to the sport. Its
publisher, Grassam, was a stationer and bookseller in Hull, who
was active as a model yachtsman and as a canoeist, a member both
of the local Kingston model yacht club and of the Humber Yawl
Association. It is rare. Copies are in the British Library and the
Bodleiean, a partial set is held in the Model Yacht Sailing
Association library and another in that of the Humber Yawl
Association. The model yachting editor throughout its life was Tom
Bruce who, with his father and other shopkeepers of the town, had
been instrumental in founding the Kingston MYC in 1881.

The magazine's original intention was to serve the model
yachting community alone, but very soon the need for a wider
circulation and better advertising income was felt and space was

offered to another thriving and Hull-based aspect of maritime sport, the Humber Yawl Association. George Holmes, a local enthusiast for single handed cruising in small sailing canoes, became canoeing editor, bringing with him additional subscribers and a small amount of advertising revenue from professional builders and others who catered to the needs of the canoeists. On this basis the magazine increased in size and in coverage and was the catalyst for the foundation of a number of model yacht clubs and for the instigation of inter-club and regional championships. The magazine continued to thrive until 1894, when Holmes relinquished his editorial chair and could not be replaced from the local canoeing community. Bruce, who was by now partner in a house furnishing business on Hessle Road, recognised that the model yachting element was not viable on its own and closed the magazine.

It appears to have had nationwide circulation through railway bookstalls as well as a direct subscription business, with some subscribers on the Continent (as far away as Baltic Russia) and in the USA, as well as in the UK.

The model yachting material contains the usual 'how to build it' articles and some discussion of design problems, together with club activity reports that are useful mainly for establishing the existence of clubs rather than for any useful information about their boats and racing practice. From the outset the magazine carried model yacht designs, some uncredited, and presumably by the editor himself, others contributed. Many are the result of design competitions that Bruce ran regularly. Most of the designs are for 10 Tonners to the '1730' Rule which was then the most common class and was used for inter-club racing. This is the first sequence of designs to a common Rule over a succession of years and thus the first to permit some assessment of design development.

Towards the end of the magazine's life Bruce decided that the Length and Sail Area Rule, adopted by full size designers in 1887, was preferable as a new standard; to this end he promoted competitions for designs to the new Rule. Most of the entries are 'transitional' between the old and the new Rules, as few of the entrants had had much experience of sailing boats to the new Rule when they drew their designs.

*236   *The Model Yachtsman* (edited by H B TUCKER):
London, monthly from April 1928.
from April 1932, as *The Model Yachtsman and Marine Models Magazine*

from April 1933, as *Marine Models (incorporating The Model Yachtsman)*.

last issue, Vol 12, No. 6, September 1939.

Continued as *Marine Models (incorporating The Model Yachtsman)*: London, Hutchinson, monthly from Vol 13, No 1, May, 1947.

From October 1947, as *Marine and Aero Models.*

last issue, June, 1948.

This title was spun off from the model yachting column in *Model Engineer* and was edited throughout its pre-war existence by Tucker, who was Secretary and subsequently Chairman of the Model Yachting Association for much of the period.

Tucker was a close associate of W J Daniels, with whom he wrote the classic *Model Sailing Craft* (No. 33) and other titles. He was the pre-eminent publicist for model yachting of the period, particularly for the activity of the Model Yachting Association itself and for the *Yachting Monthly* Cup international competition for 'A' Class yachts.

It quickly became clear that the market for a journal of model yachting alone was insufficient and the coverage was expanded to include all forms of boat modelling. To reflect this the title was changed in 1933. Even so, keeping the magazine afloat required a struggle, for both readers and contributions. Though Tucker wrote extensively himself, and occasionally anonymously in an attempt to stir up controversy, he claimed that he had never rejected a contributed piece. After the death of E E Marshall, a businessman and prominent model yachtsman, who had acted as publisher and allowed the magazine to operate from his London offices (and possibly subsidised it in other ways), Tucker was hard put to keep going. In 1939 he was seeking to dispose of the title when the declaration of war in September offered him an honourable reason to close down for the duration. It did not resume in its previous form.

The premises from which it had been edited were destroyed in the blitz and the goodwill of the title was disposed of to

Hutchinson. After the war, the Hutchinson version of *Marine Models* picked up the volume numbering where Tucker had left off.

Despite its financial problems, the magazine in its original form was clearly the journal of record for the Model Yachting Association and for the sport generally. Its September number each year included extended coverage of the 'A' Class Championship races and the international races for the *Yachting Monthly* Cup. It regularly published designs for most of the popular classes. Many of these are by the leading designers of the day and a number of classic boats first appeared in its pages. Though the magazine drawings were intended as promotions for the sale of full size plans, they are in a relatively large format and it is perfectly possible to enlarge them and build from them. Many readers may well have done just that, as the blueprints cost between two and three times as much as the very similar offerings from the competing *English Mechanic*. Over the years the magazine included a large collection of good half tone illustrations of boats, venues and competitors.

The post war continuation attempted to pursue a similar policy to that of its pre-war antecedent, carrying reports of Model Yachting Association general meetings, and a small amount of design and construction material. The slow return of model yachting to its pre-war levels of activity meant that there was not a lot to report.

The costs of a fully commercial operation were such that it was quickly expanded to cover aircraft modelling as well but, even so, could not make a go of it. It carried a number of authoritative articles by Charles Farley on model yachting in the USA, which provided a means for British skippers to catch up on what had been done there during the war, including the development of the vane gear. A comprehensive survey of the vane gear and its use was cut short by the closure of the title. Despite this, a few years later, when the vane was coming into general use in Britain, even some of the keenest skippers were unaware of this source of information.

*237   *MYA News* **(edited originally by F C TANSLEY):
Hove, Model Yachting Association: Bi-monthly
from January 1947.
various changes of periodicity, editor and
location.
last issue, No 143, 1974.**

This was a long lived, if extremely variable, in-house production by
the MYA. It grew out of the Hove MYC's *Lagoon Times,* also edited
by Tansley. A couple of free copies went to each club, and
additional copies could be had against payment. The format,
periodicity and production varied considerably over the years, from
as little as one or two cyclostyled sheets to a decently printed 32
page monthly booklet and back again.

The farewell number claimed that the journal had reached its
apogee in 1953-55, under the editorship of Major G B Lee and this
seems, from the partial run that we have seen, to be the case. It
was during this period that it was most comprehensive and best
produced. Even then, when paid subscriptions were at their peak,
the number of paying subscribers was very small, averaging less
than three sales per club, It was thus always a drain on the
finances of the association and would have had to at least double
its paid circulation to break even. Editors regularly complained
that in some clubs the Secretary made no effort even to pass on the
free copies to members.

Lee and a number of other editors died in harness, possibly
because potential replacements were, very reasonably, reluctant to
come forward while the incumbent still breathed.

We have been able to consult only a mixed group of issues.
The contents are mainly given over to race reports and information
on the decisions of Council, with only very few articles of wider
interest. The letters columns occasionally contain useful material,
but also a disproportionate number of carping critics of the
administration.

The role of *MYA News* was to an extent continued by the
production of a regular *Acquaint* (again in varying format and
periodicity) to pass essential information from the Council to clubs,
and more recently by the practice of copying Council minutes to
clubs.

In mid-1999 The *Acquaint* has expanded to a larger magazine
format, but is still distributed only to clubs.

238   *Radio Control Boat Modeler*: US journal, no detail available.

When *Radio Control Model Boating* (No.240) ceased publication, Rod Carr's column transferred to this title and changed its masthead to 'Strictly Sail'. In 1973, the column was taken over by Don Prough and Rod's work moved to *Model Builder* and subsequently to *US Boat and Ship Modeler*.

239   *Radio Control Boat Modeler*: US journal, no publication detail. Monthly from 1991.

We have not seen any of this journal. It is a separate enterprise from the preceding entry and carries the more recent of Rod Carr's long series of articles on radio yachting under the aegis of the AMYA.

240   *Radio Control Model Boating*: US journal, no publication details: early 1970s, ceased publication by mid 1973.

This journal carried the nascent AMYA's column, transferred from *Model Boating World News*, under the title 'R/C Sail Activity', written by Rod Carr and covering, among other matter, the early ACCRs (in UK English, National Championships) run by the AMYA .

Radio Yachting News
see *Model Yachting News* (No. 231).

RailRoad Model Craftsman
see *Model Craftsman* (No. 218).

241   *RC Marine*: St Fargeau, Editions Techniques et Loisirs: Monthly from April 1991.

We have not seen this.

Aimed at the popular end of the model boat market, this magazine has always included coverage of radio sailing activity. Despite attracting contributions from many of the leading French exponents, our informants regard it as a bit lightweight. There is a plans service and a few Marblehead and 1-metre designs have been included.

242   *The Rudder* (originally edited by T F DAY): New York, The Rudder Publishing Company: Monthly from 1890.

This magazine seems to have been directed, like its British contemporary *Yachting and Boating Monthly,* at least in part to owners of boats smaller than the 'first class' yachts that so obsessed most journals of the day. It published practical material on design and building, some of which was collected in book form (*The Schooner Book, The Racer Book, The Catboat Book* etc,)

In its early years, *The Rudder* carried a fair amount of material on model sailing, much of it drawn from the activity of the clubs in the New York area, particularly those that sailed on the lake in Prospect Park, Brooklyn. Designs came from a wider range of contributors, including some from Britain. A lot of this appeared in collected form in Fisher's *How to Build a Model Yacht* (No 46). The BL (SRIS) has a run from 1910 to 1928.

243   *Die Seekiste. Zietschrift fur Föderung des Schiffsmodellbaus. Herausgeben mit Unterstutzung des Oberkommandos der Kriegsmarine*: Berlin, Matthiesen, Monthly from April 1941.
Last issue, September 1944.

We have seen no actual copies of this title. It was a magazine, published with the support of the German navy, designed to instil patriotic and practical virtues in the young by way of ship modelling.

The index for 1943 shows a fair amount of model yacht matter, including plans by **de Bruycker** and Hans Scherpinski, together with articles on de B's favourite building techniques and on 'building without plywood', that may suggest that shortages of materials were beginning to be felt by this stage of the war. Our advisers draw attention to the emphasis on sailing models as reflecting difficulties by that stage of the war with the supply of small electric motors and batteries for powered models.

The activity reports imply that a programme of *Gau* and *Länd* championships for model yachts was being organised for the first time in 1943.

Ships and Ship Models
see *Model Ships and Power Boats* (No. 224)

244   *Schiffsmodell*: Villingen-Schwenningen, Neckar-Verlag, Bi-monthly from January, 1978; monthly from January 1988.

A spin off from Neckar's earlier title *Modell*, which had carried minimal amounts of sailing model material, *Schiffsmodell* has varied in the amount of coverage given to sailing models over the years. From the outset, until about 1991, there was a regular flow of material on designs and construction for current competitive radio sailing from **F K Ries**, who also published a number of handbooks on the subject. There were also some designs, including some contributed from France, Australia and the USA.

As the German competitive scene became more active, a number of the leading participants contributed, including Gerd Mentges, Horst Krönke and Thomas Dreyer. Chris Jackson has also written fairly regularly for them, mainly on international meetings and developments in the international organisation of the sport.

245   *Der Segelsport*: Berlin, monthly from April 1914 to January 1923 and from April 1925 to December 1926.

A magazine of full size sailing, a competitor to *Die Yacht*, but much less solidly based. Quite apart from its cessation as a result of the 1923 inflation, its content fluctuated wildly between 200 and 1600 pages a year. Despite (or perhaps because of) its vicissitudes, *Der Segelsport* carried a good deal of model yachting material by writers such as Paul Krüge and **Emil Zwalgun** and, we are told by those familiar with both, is to be preferred to *Die Yacht* as a source for model yachting in Germany in the 1920s. It contains material on the development of the Berlin *Sonderklasse* models, which were similar in concept to the 30 Square metre 'Skerry Cruiser' class in the full size arena. This class was eventually adopted as the DSV Class C.

246   *Tribord Amures; pour le Propagation de l'Idée Maritime par la Construction de Modèles de Bateaux* (edited by Gussy JAMBIERS): Brussels, MYC de Bruxelles, monthly from January 1945.

This entry was noted from a French bibliographical source. We know no more about it, not even how long it survived. It deserves inclusion, if only in recognition of the huge effort of will required to produce a new magazine, however slight, while the war was still in progress and within four months of the liberation of Brussels in the previous September. There does not appear to be a copy in the Belgian Royal Library.

247 *The Turning Pole*: London, The Vintage Model
Yacht Group, by subscription: Irregular, from
1992.

This occasional journal had a prior existence as *The VMYG
Newsletter*, from 1988. Originally it was little more than a
calendar of events and administrative trivia, but it has now grown
to include reports of VG meetings and occasional articles on the
restoration of individual boats and on the researches being carried
out by members.

There are also snippets from the past, giving details of
construction and rigging practice appropriate to older styles of
model. Despite its longer existence, it has yet to develop as healthy
a flow of contributions as its American counterpart, *The Model
Yacht* (No. 226).

248 *US Boat and Ship Modeller* (edited by William C
Northrop Jr.): Newport Beach, CA, CMB Inc:
Quarterly from Summer, 1976.

Last issue, 1996

This general marine modelling title became the home for Rod
Carr's 'Strictly Sail' column from the Summer 1987 issue. The
opening article contains a brief organisational history of AMYA and
its origins as a breakaway group from MYRAA. Thereafter. the
content is much the same as in the *Model Builder* series, with a
sprinkling of designs to the Marblehead, 10-rater and other classes
and a good photo coverage of the US competitive scene. We have
seen copies of the series up to 1993, but it continued until the
magazine closed down.

249   *Work, an Illustrated Magazine of Practice and Theory for all Workmen, Professional and Amateur*: London, Cassell, weekly from 21 March, 1889.

From 18 October 1924, amalgamated with The *Amateur Mechanic* as *The Amateur Mechanic and Work*: London, weekly.

From 29 October 1926, amalgamated *with The English Mechanic* as *English and Amateur Mechanics*: London, Rolls House, for the proprietors, Gilbert Wood & Co., New Series, weekly.

From 4 January 1929 *as English Mechanics.*

From 1 May 1942, as *Mechanics.*

From July 1956, as *Home Mechanics.*

from April 1959, incorporated in *Model Engineer.*

We cannot claim to have examined all the issues of this long lived weekly technical journal, which passed through many guises and followed varying editorial policies over the years.

For a long period in the 19th century it seems to have aimed predominantly at professional artisans but, even then, contained occasional matter on leisure crafts appropriate to the better class of working man, including model sailing craft.

None of this seems to relate closely to what we know of the activity of organised model yachtsmen, and much appears in the form of brief answers to readers' queries, which were a regular feature of most of this 'popular mechanics' breed of journal. In this forum, the information is sketchy in the extreme and usually contributed by the very small editorial team, which seldom, if ever, contained active model yachtsmen. Thus, replies to queries tend to be out of date and often distinctly impractical. Some of this material is re-used in *Cassell's Cyclopaedia of Mechanics* (No.63). The very few contributed articles that we have come across in the earlier volumes have at least the advantage of being written by active practitioners, but seldom by competitive model yachtsmen. Though more practical, they are often technically out of date.

Only for a period in the 1930s did the editorial policy of *English Mechanics*, as it then was, swing firmly to serving the amateur model engineer and home constructor, rather than the professional artisan. The magazine thus became a direct competitor to the *Model Engineer*, with articles on live steam model locomotive construction by the ubiquitous contributor who wrote under the pseudonym of 'LBSC', and other comparable material.

As part of this policy, it introduced a model yachting section. This was largely conducted by two members of the Gosport club. One was a gentleman amateur who wrote under the pseudonym of 'Lilliput', who has not yet been identified. The other was the designer Reg W Lance, who was responsible for the lines of *Flame*, which won the *Yachting Monthly* Cup in 1935. He contributed a series of elegant and up to date designs for each of the classes, together with series on the design process and on the design and construction of fittings.

Internal evidence, and the highly finished presentation of his drawings, suggests that Lance was by profession a draughtsman, probably in one of the yacht yards of the Gosport area. He was no great hand with a pen, but in his commentary on design developments and new ideas that he has seen, he shows himself to have an incisive technical mind.

There are some other contributors, including E B Savage, a civil engineer whose model yachting connections we have not yet identified, who wrote a long and very competent sequence on hull construction. After the start of the war in 1939, the magazine necessarily shrinks and the model yachting content disappears.

250   *Die Yacht*: **Berlin, Wedekind, weekly in summer, fortnightly in winter from July 1904.**
from 1912, weekly throughout the year.

from the early 1920s, Berlin, Delius, Klasing.

Break of publication from 1943.

Resumes 1950: Bielefeldt, Delius Klasing, monthly. From 1951, fortnightly.

There is a part run of this title, from 1904 to 1931, in the BL (SRIS). During the period we have so far been able to examine, it covered full size yachting, both sail and power, in some detail There is good coverage of design developments in sailing yachts to the International Rule of 1907, as well as to local German Rules.

In the pre 1914 period there is no regular coverage of model yachting, but a very few articles that give some idea of the scope and style of the sport in Germany. There is occasional coverage to model sailing through the 1930s, for instance reporting the substantial civic and Party celebrations associated with the opening in Berlin in 1938 of what was claimed to be the first purpose-built model yacht lake in Germany.

After its 1950 resumption, model yachting gets some coverage in the period 1955-65, largely of the activity of the Pollhän brothers and Jacobsen in Hamburg and their links with the British model yachting scene. There are also occasional designs, for example by **de Bruycker** and Walter Nissen. Full size copies of these plans were available through DSV.

251   *Le Yacht/ Journal de la Navigation de Plaisance*:
        Paris, monthly from 1878.
        Publication ceased 1914-19 and for a period
        during the Second World War.

        1884-1952, as *Le Yacht/ Journal de la Marine.*

        1952-1961, as *Le Yacht.*

        From 1962, as *Le Yacht et le Motonautisme.*

Though long lived, this journal has had to cover a very wide range of interests. As well as the premier French yachting journal, it was also, as its title indicates, for a long period a journal of record for the French shipping industry and a vehicle for material on naval technology. We have not located a complete run in Britain, but the BL (SRIS) has copies from 1910 to 1928.

In these, among so much other material, there is not a lot of space for model yachting, but the pre-1914 issues contain some indication of the extent and nature of model sailing in France at that time, though they tend to discuss styles of sailing that seem out of date compared to what was going on in the UK at the same time. We believe that there is little model coverage after 1920.

*252   *Yachting*: **New York, Yachting Publishing Co.,**
        Monthly from 1907.
This American magazine of full size sailing carried a good deal of model yachting material during the 1920s, much of it centring round the Daniels challenge of 1921 and the subsequent development of the *Yachting Monthly* Cup competition which, among other things, prompted the foundation of MYRAA. This coverage is driven in part by the editor's interest in the use of models as trial horses for full size design, in part by the desire of modellers, particularly in the New York area, to publicise their activity.

Over the years there are accounts of US developments and their views on the international competitions in which they took part, together with discussion of the appropriateness or otherwise of full size Rating Rules for model use. Unfortunately much of this is from the pen of the pompous, opinionated and often wrongheaded John O Berg of the Central Park club. There are also construction articles by E O Bull (a superlative craftsman), by **Darling** and by **Moore** (these last being dry runs for their respective books, No. 38 and No. 99). There are a number of designs from a small range of designers, mainly for the bigger classes, such as the MYRAA Class B and for the YM 6-metre.

Model yacht coverage starts to fade away in the early 1930s and almost the last item of interest includes the earliest published lines plan for a Marblehead, which appeared early in 1932.

There was an entirely separate magazine of the same title published in New York from 1894 to 1898. We have not seen it and have no information whether it contained any coverage of model yachting

*253   *Yachting and Boating Monthly*: **London, monthly from 1906.**
later as *Yachting Monthly*.

This journal has been through several changes of policy and coverage over the years. In its early years, particularly while Herbert Reiach and Malden Heckstall-Smith were successively editor, it aimed to give comprehensive coverage to the whole of the racing scene, in direct competition with the other yachting journals and with *The Field*, though with more emphasis on the smaller classes.

Heckstall-Smith was among those who cherished the hope that models could be used to develop full size designs. He also had his differences with the YRA, and with his brother, who was its Secretary, over the suitability of the International Rule for smaller yachts. He was a founder and moving spirit in the competing Boat Racing Asociation (BRA). During the 1914-18 war he encouraged model yachtsmen to build models to the BRA 18-footer Rule. After the war, aided and abetted by Bill Daniels, he turned to models as a field in which to develop his ideas on alternatives to the International Rule.

In its early years *YM* gave substantial coverage to model yachting, carrying important articles on design and construction by H Hardy Simpson before 1914 and several important design contributions by Alfred Turner during and immediately after the 1914 war.

In the early twenties, reflecting the association between Daniels and the editor, it carried almost blow by blow coverage to Bill's 1922 foray to the USA and the subsequent development of the *Yachting Monthly* Cup competition and its associated '*YM* 6-metre Rule'. The early annual competitions are reported in detail, as are the conflicts between the MYA and the Scottish MYA over the way the 'British Empire selection races' should be run.

This fades away very promptly after the foundation of *The Model Yachtsman* in 1928, and there is no significant material after a report on the *YM* Cup races of 1929. At about the same time Maurice Griffiths became editor and the magazine changed its direction to devote most of its coverage to cruising in small yachts. There is no very significant model yachting coverage thereafter.

*253   *Yachting Monthly*: London, monthly, from January 1898; last issue, December, 1898
This was a short lived magazine that aimed to serve the growing market of those who owned and raced small open keelboats and dinghies as well as the 'first class' yachts with which *The Field* was largely concerned. It contains some priceless detail on the light weight construction techniques developed by Linton Hope for his mould-breaking small raters and an important article by John Odgers on model yachting at Kensington. This includes a lines plan for a crack boat said to date from 1863 and those of several contemporary 10-raters by members of the Model Yacht Sailing Association, as well as material on his perception of the social divisions between the club and its neighbours of the London MYC.

254   *Yachting World*: London, Iliffe, weekly from 1894: switch to monthly in 1930s, still in issue.
We have not had an opportunity to search this journal for model yachting material.

*255   *The Yachtsman*: London, weekly from 25 April, 1891: after 1945, a switch to monthly, and then quarterly, publication; last issue 1966.
One of the 'new journals' of the late 19th century, this weekly made wide use of photogravure technology to include a high proportion of photo illustrations.

Because it was a weekly, there was a lot of space to fill and, from the outset, model yachtsmen used it to report their race results and club business meetings. There was a ready flow of this sort of information and, within the first year, a series of letters from G T Sanderson, by then the Grand Old Man of London model yachting. These are the sole source for the sailing of the artisans who used the Green Park reservoir in the 1820s, and for a number of technical aspects of the sailing practice of the mid century.

From the mid 1890s there are occasional designs, usually in the context of reporting remarkable successes, (e.g., Paxton's *Silver Spray* in 1893). The designing competitions that are a regular feature attract a number of entries (some of them successful) from men known to be active as model yachtsmen; in 1907 there is a competition specifically for 12-metre models to the then new International Rule.

In 1908 a series of articles on model yachting, 'by an expert' is clearly written by a member of one of the clubs using the Round Pond. Though some of the potential authors can be eliminated by means of internal evidence, and it is almost certain that the writer was a member of Model Yachting Sailing Association rather than the London, it has not been possible to make a positive identification. The series includes a brief history of design developments as seen from London and a number of designs by the leading designers of the day, including Paxton and John Odgers. This last is the 10-r *Buttercup*, owned by George Braine, the boat on which Braine developed his automatic steering gear.[14] As is often the case with such material in magazines of wider audience, the series peters out without a conclusion and without including all the material on fittings and the like that is promised.

We have not so far had the opportunity to examine this title after mid 1910.

256 *The Yachtsman's Gazette*: **London, Monthly from February 1854.**
last issue, December, 1854.

A journal started by a yachtsman who, it seems, could not get his contributions into the journals that then covered the sport. The first, and only, volume contains a fair amount on the activity of two clubs which called themselves model yacht clubs, the London MYC and the Birkenhead MYC, but deals mainly with their activity in the sailing of what were, for the period, small manned craft on the Thames and the Mersey respectively. We know from other sources that both these clubs had concurrent activity sailing true model yachts, but there is nothing to show whether the Mersey club was as sharply divided between model and full size sailors as that in London.

It does however, also contain the preface to the London MYC's original Rules of 1846. This is a grandiloquent piece of maritime patriotism, but among other things makes clear that the club was originally established to sail model yachts on the Serpentine.

---

[14] This boat survives, as does the original Braine gear.

CURVED AIR PRESS

Send orders to Russell Potts, Curved Air Press, 8 Sherard Road, London, SE9 6EP.

Overseas orders must be paid by Sterling cheque or bankers draft drawn on London. Please add realistic airmail postage costs. Make cheques payable to R R Potts

The titles marked * are also available from **Sails, etc.,** who can offer a Visa or Mastercard payment facility

141 High Street, Kelvedon, Essex, CO5 9AA.

Tel/Fax: +44 (0) 1376 571 437

Titles Available, 1999

VMYG Reprints

These are card covered Xerox reproductions of ephemeral publications of model yachting interest from the past.

1 YOUR MODEL YACHT: How to Sail it; Practical Hints for the Young Novice: by A Member of One of the Leading Model Yacht Clubs:1929 (?).

ISBN:1 873148 00 3: A5: 12pp: £3.00 plus 30p P&P in the UK.

A simple pamphlet aimed at schoolboys, dealing with the sailing of the simplest models without steering gear, or with weighted rudders.

2 HOW TO SAIL YOUR MODEL YACHT

Bassett-Lowke: 1930s.

ISBN:1 873148 01 1: A5: 12pp: £3.00 plus 30p P&P in the UK.

A more sophisticated pamphlet written originally in the 1930s to accompany Bassett's superior toy yachts. Deals with the use of Braine gear.

3 TUNING UP A MODEL YACHT:

D A MacDonald: MAP: 1957.

ISBN:1 873148 02 X: A5:16pp: £3.00 plus 40p P&P in the UK.

More sophisticated again. Aims at the competitive model yachtsman and assumes that the boat is fitted with vane gear.

4 THE MODEL DOCKYARD HANDY-BOOK:

The Model Dockyard, Fleet St: 4th Edition:1872 With a new introduction by Russell Potts: ISBN:1 873148 03 8: oblong A4: 76pp: £10.00 plus £1.30 P&P in the UK.

A comprehensive catalogue and guide to construction from one of the leading model engineering firms of the mid 19th century, founded in 1779. As well as model yachts it covers an extensive range of steam and clockwork powered model boats as well as model steam engines and railway locomotives, together with parts and castings for home construction.

Practical Guides for Vintage Modellers

* JACK'S GUIDE TO THE RESTORATION OF OLDER MODEL YACHTS

Jack Drury, with commentary and interpolations by Russell Potts and Richard Howlett. ISBN 1 873148 09 7. A5: 32pp. £6 plus 50p P&P in the UK.

A guide to the techniques required to bring old wooden boats back to sailing condition. Draws on the experience of a modeller active since the 1920s and of two of today's most experienced restorers.

*BUILDING PLANKED MODELS: A Manual of Vintage Model Yacht Construction.

Charles H Farley, edited by Earl Boebert, Afterword by Rod Carr. A4: 114 pp : £15 plus £1.50 P&P in the UK.

This is a reprint by the USVMYG of articles that originally appeared in 1945 in *Model Yachting Monthly*, the magazine of the MYRAA, which Farley edited.

The material has been re-organised to give a more coherent presentation than was possible in its original form as disparate articles, but apart from this and a few footnotes what you get is what he wrote.

The techniques described represent the normal technology of the period. The methods are clearly described and, so far as any written text can tell you how to do it, will permit a reasonably careful and assiduous beginner to successfully complete a boat.

Rod Carr's Afterword touches briefly on how to up-date these methods for modern materials and glues.

Model Yachting History

* "M" 1930-1990: A Design History of the Marblehead Class of Model Yacht.

by Russell Potts: ISBN: 1 873148 04 6: A5: 24 pp: £4.00. plus 50p P&P in the UK.

Covers the long story of the 'M' from its origins in the USA to its present world wide distribution. Seeks to explain how and why the shape of boats has changed. Many lines drawings.

* 100 YEARS OF THE 10-RATER RULE

by Russell Potts: ISBN: 1 873148 05 4: A5:18pp: £4.00 plus
50p P&P in the UK.

> Despite the title, this souvenir of the 1987
> Centenary 10-r Worlds in Gothenburg deals only
> with design developments before the introduction
> of radio control. Line and photo illustrations.

SPORTING HOBBIES AND SOCIAL CLASS: the case of
Model Yachting by Russell Potts: 1988, A4; 12pp. £5.00 plus
50p P&P in the UK.

> A survey of the social background of Victorian
> model yachtsmen, concentrating on two episodes
> involving clubs sailing on water in the Royal
> Parks of London.

Not Model Yachting History

THE SOCIAL CONSTRUCTION OF A LEISURE TECHNOLOGY: YACHT DESIGN AND THE RATING RULES 1880-1920

by Russell Potts 1995 A4: 70pp : £10.00 plus £1.50p P&P
in the UK.

This is not a model yachting title, but the text of
the M.Sc dissertation I wrote a couple of years
ago. Vast erudition combined with original ideas
about the taxonomy of sports, the ideology of the
Victorian yachtsman and the way in which
technology is shaped by social aims of the users.
Lots of lines plans of Victorian racing yachts.

Forthcoming

Forthcoming

LET'S PUT THE RACE ON RIGHT HERE!

A picture history of model yacht ponds.

By Russell Potts

This has been squeezed out for the present by work on the Bibliography. It will come eventually.

* RALPH'S GUIDE TO VINTAGE SAILMAKING

Ralph Nellist, a textile technologist, has spent the years since he joined the Vintage Group researching sail cloths and sail making techniques. His work can now stand comparison with the best professional products of the 1930s. He is (slowly) committing what he has learned to paper and we shall eventually be proud to publish what will be the standard work.